SEAL THE DEAL & LET'S BOOGIE

Music transcriptions by Pete Billmann and Jeff Jacobson

ISBN 978-4950-7092-1

HAL•LEONARD®
CORPORATION
7777 W. BLUEMOUND RD. P.O. BOX 13819 MILWAUKEE, WI 53213

Visit Hal Leonard Online at
www.halleonard.com

The Devil's Bleeding Crown

Words and Music by Michael Poulsen

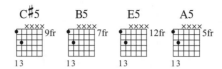

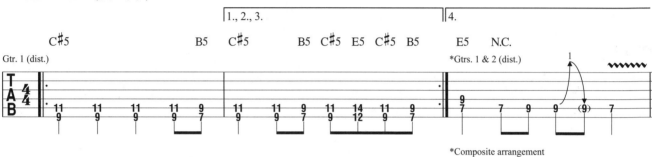

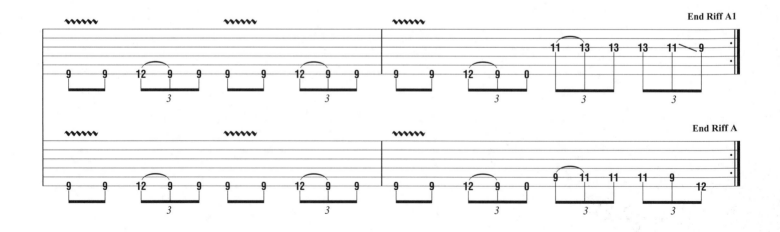

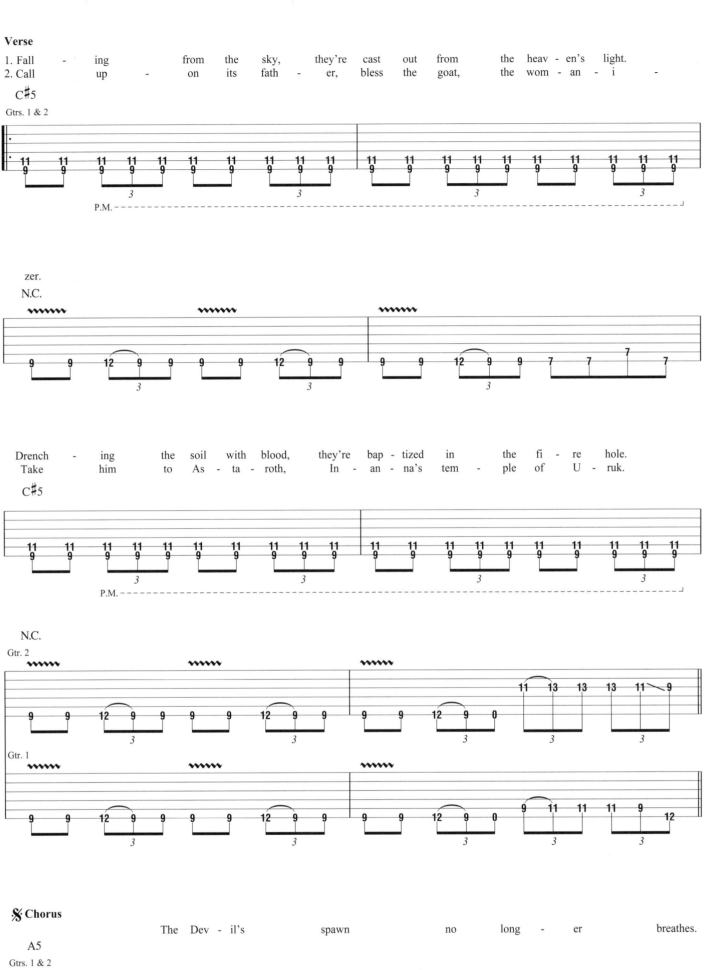

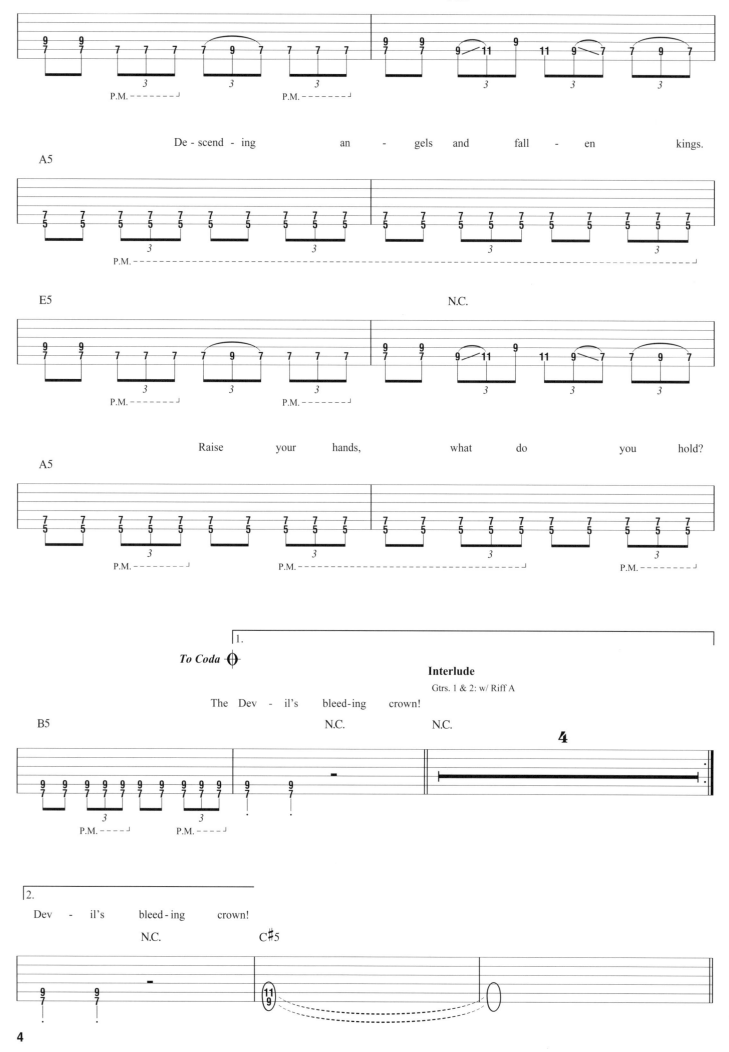

Interlude

N.C.

Gtr. 2

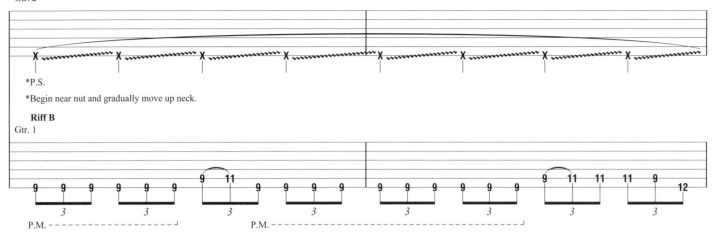

*P.S.

*Begin near nut and gradually move up neck.

Riff B

Gtr. 1

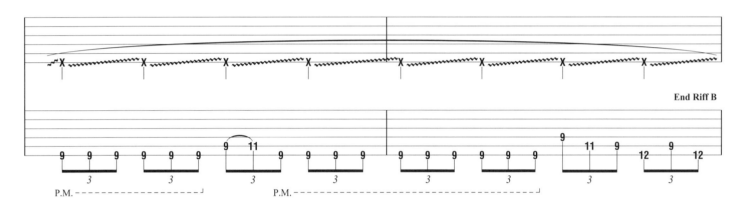

Gtr. 1: w/ Riff B (3 times)

Gtr. 2

Gtrs. 1 & 2: w/ Riff B (2 times)

N.C.

Gtr. 3 (dist.)

P.S.

Guitar Solo

B5

Gtr. 3

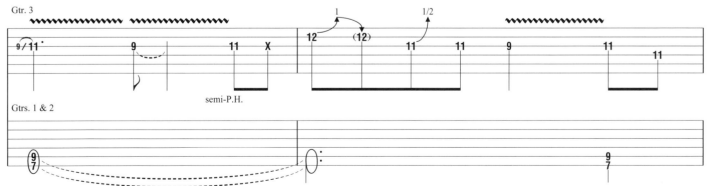

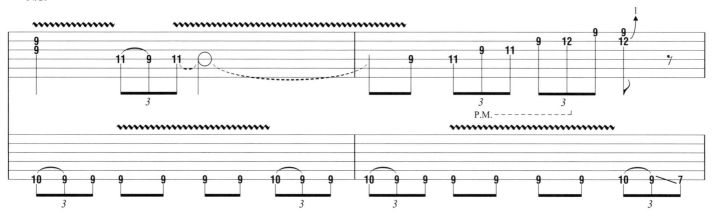

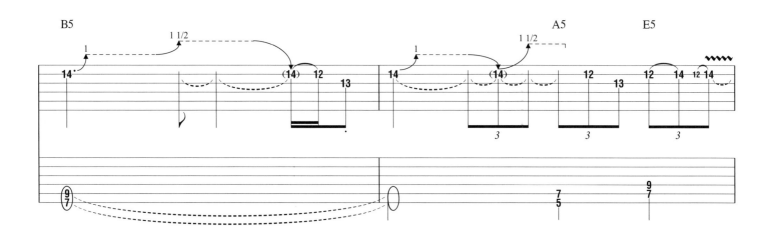

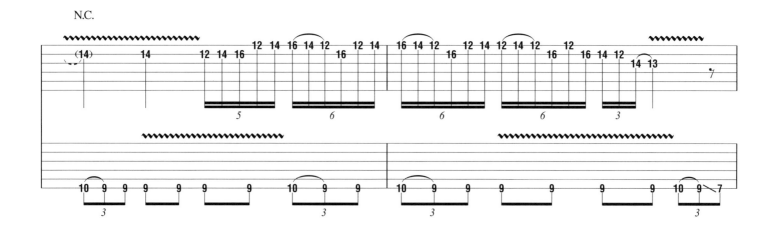

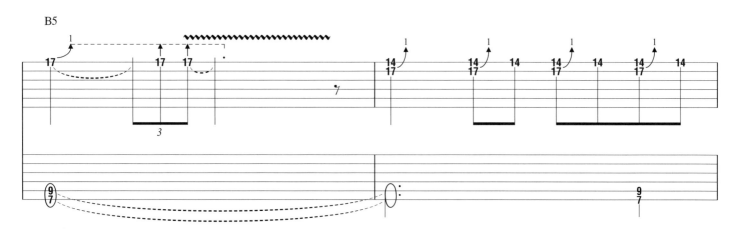

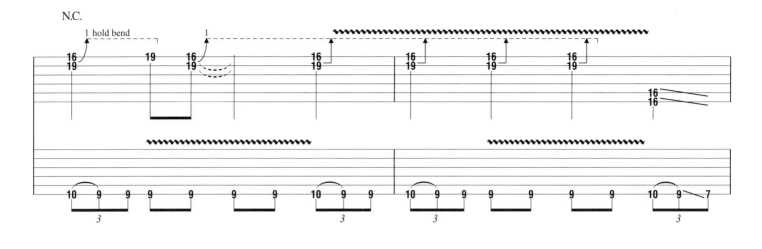

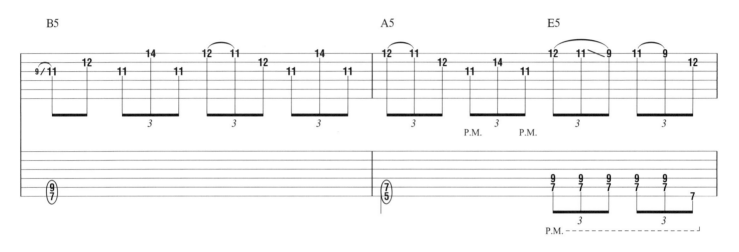

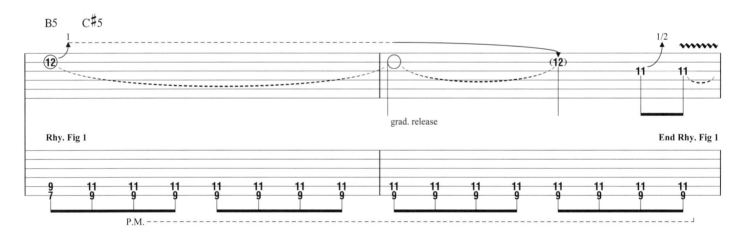

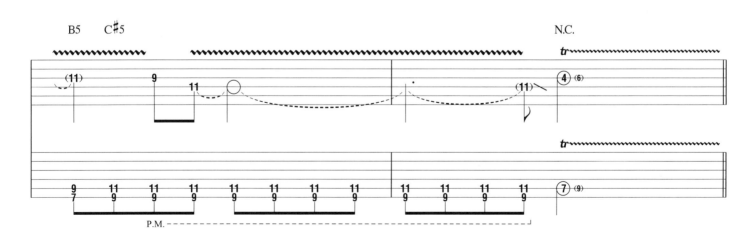

Bridge

Gtrs. 1 & 2: w/ Rhy. Fig. 1 (3 times)
Gtr. 3 tacet

B5   C#5

They gath-ered all the chil - dren out - side the church,

B5   C#5

and nev - er would they know what went down in there.

B5   C#5

Close the door and hear all the an - gels scream,

"Oh, mer - cy, mer - cy, mer-cy, oh, mer - cy, please."

B5   C#5   N.C.

Gtrs. 1 & 2

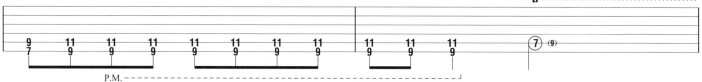

Down, down, down,

B5   C#5

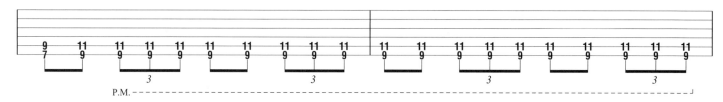

down be - low you can hear his hoof dig-ging through the ground.

B5   C#5

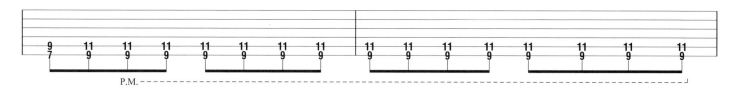

Oh, Lord, Lord, Lord,

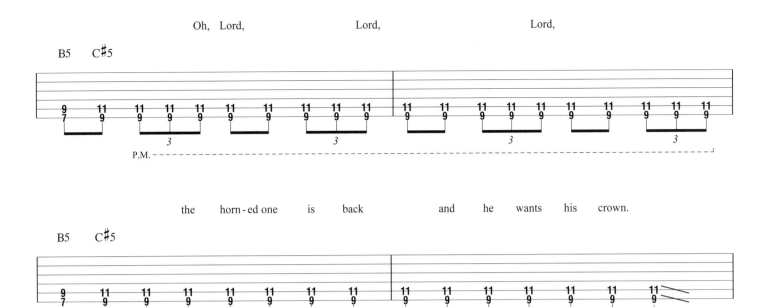

the horn-ed one is back and he wants his crown.

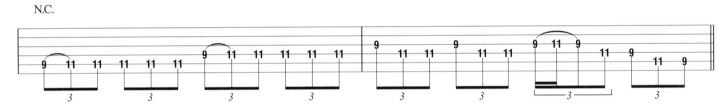

D.S. al Coda

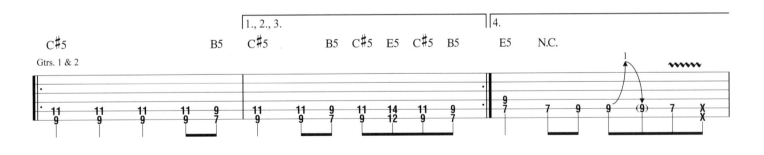

⊕ **Coda**

Outro
Gtrs. 1 & 2: w/ Riffs A & A1

Dev - il's bleed - ing crown!

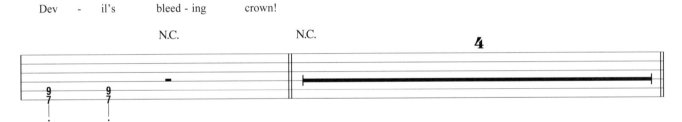

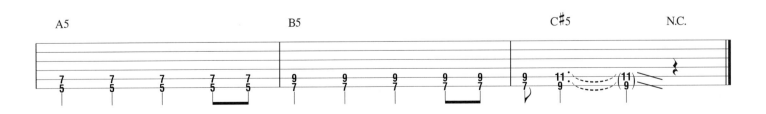

Marie Laveau

Words and Music by Michael Poulsen

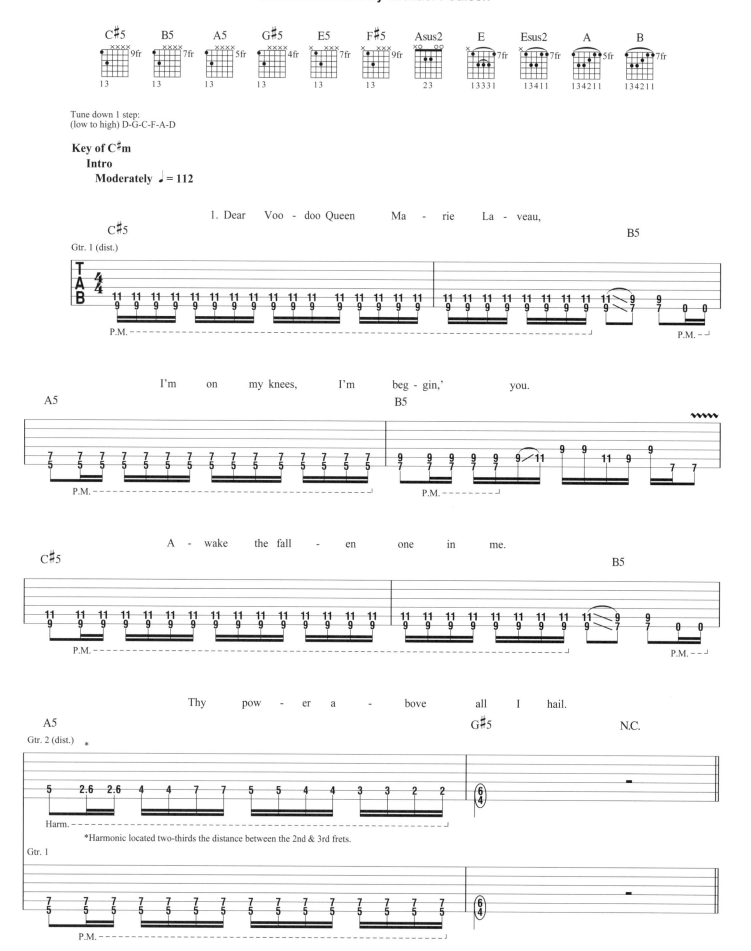

Tune down 1 step:
(low to high) D-G-C-F-A-D

Key of C#m
Intro
Moderately ♩ = 112

Verse

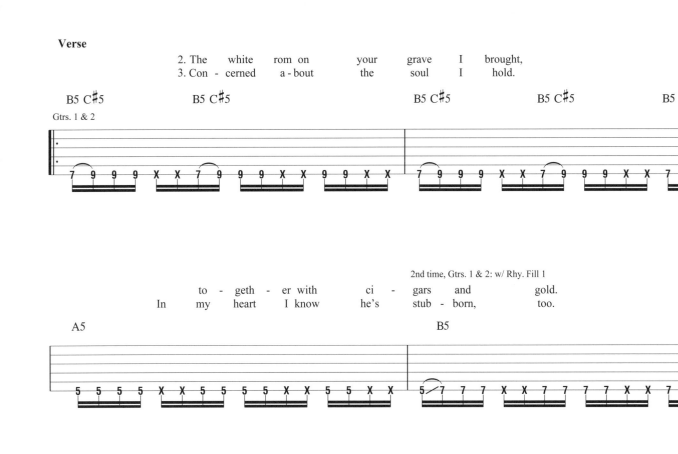

2. The white rom on your grave I brought,
3. Con - cerned a - bout the soul I hold.

to - geth - er with ci - gars and gold.
In my heart I know he's stub - born, too.

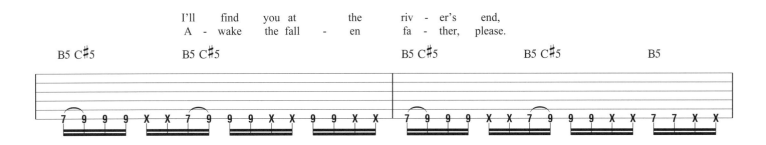

I'll find you at the riv - er's end,
A - wake the fall - en fa - ther, please.

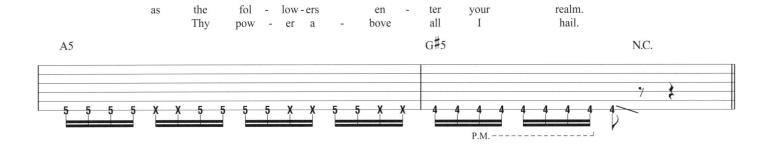

as the fol - low - ers en - ter your realm.
Thy pow - er a - bove all I hail.

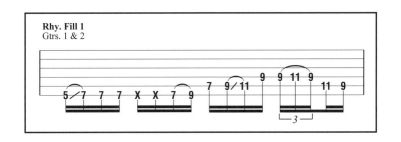

Rhy. Fill 1
Gtrs. 1 & 2

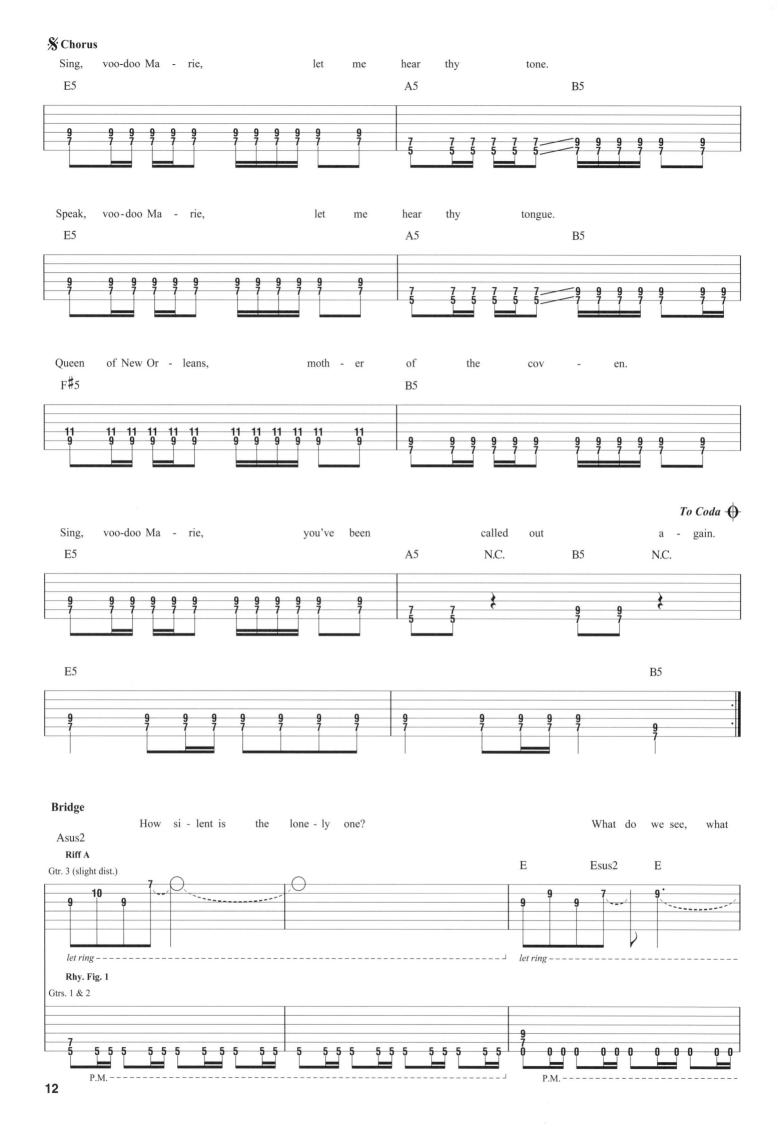

do we know?   Ma - rie La-veau, I'm full of hope.

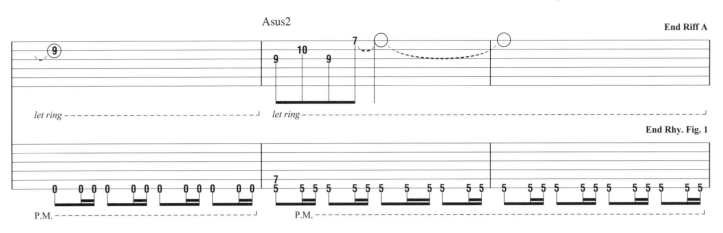

Asus2   **End Riff A**

End Rhy. Fig. 1

Gtr. 3 tacet

Let me speak un - til for - ev - er more.

B5

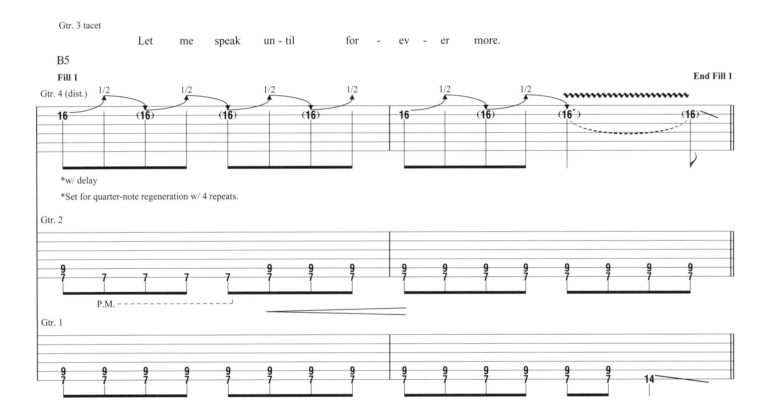

Fill 1   **End Fill 1**

Gtr. 4 (dist.)

*w/ delay

*Set for quarter-note regeneration w/ 4 repeats.

Gtr. 2

Gtr. 1

Interlude

Gtr. 4 tacet

*E

Gtr. 2

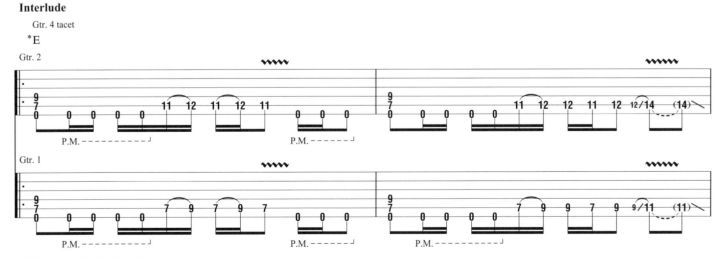

Gtr. 1

*Chord symbols reflect basic harmony.

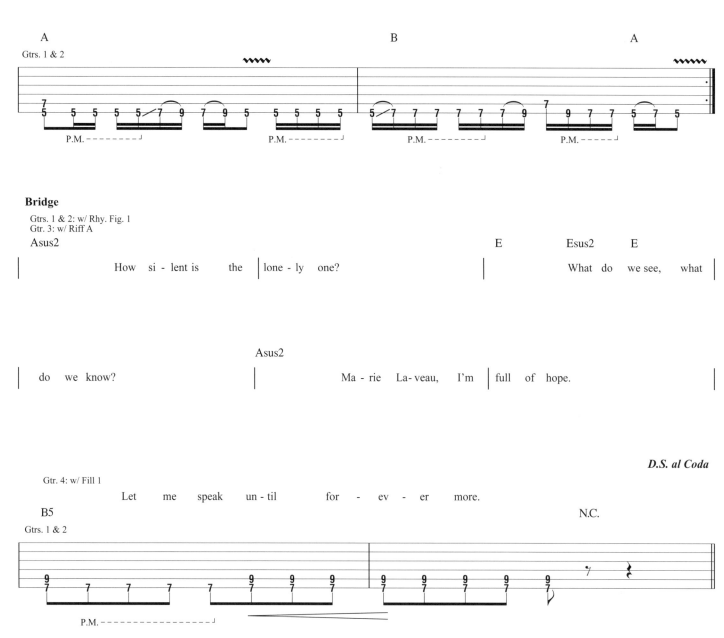

Bridge

Gtrs. 1 & 2: w/ Rhy. Fig. 1
Gtr. 3: w/ Riff A

Asus2   **E   Esus2   E**

How si - lent is the | lone - ly one?   What do we see, what

                      Asus2

do we know? | Ma - rie La - veau, I'm | full of hope.

D.S. al Coda

Gtr. 4: w/ Fill 1

Let me speak un - til for - ev - er more.

B5   **N.C.**

Gtrs. 1 & 2

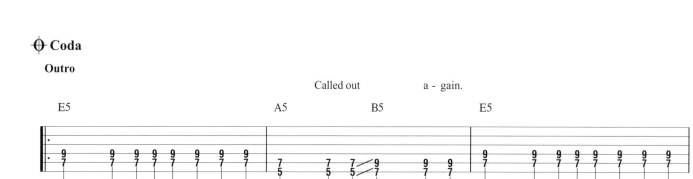

⊕ Coda

Outro

Called out   a - gain.

E5   **A5**   **B5**   **E5**

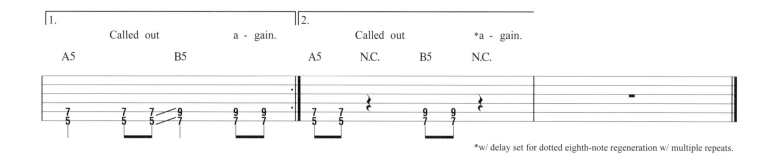

1.
Called out   a - gain.

2.
Called out   *a - gain.

A5   **B5**   **A5   N.C.   B5   N.C.**

*w/ delay set for dotted eighth-note regeneration w/ multiple repeats.

The Bliss

Words and Music by Michael Poulsen

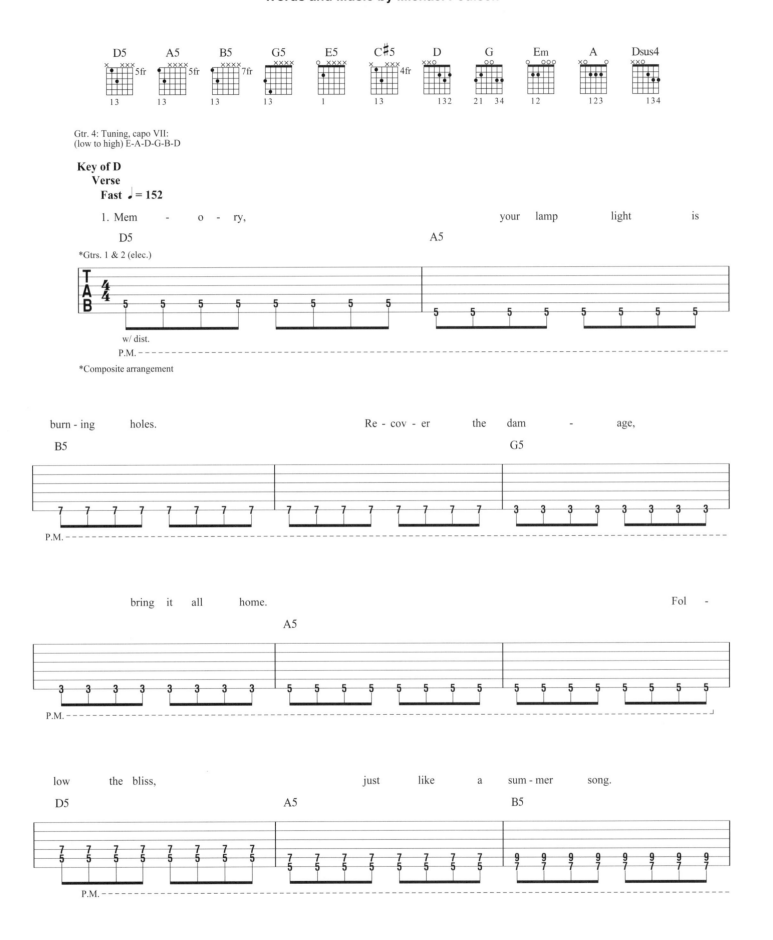

Please stay there for - ev - er, I'll try to re -

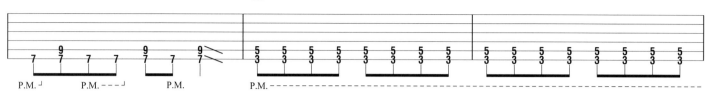

mem - ber. Come home.

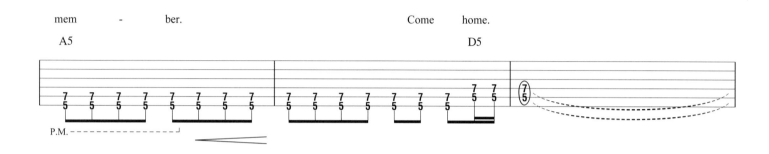

Verse

2. Mem - o - ry, you gave me an - oth - er note, a voice that is
3. Hap - pi - ness, I'm sor - ry you've been on hold. The doors will be

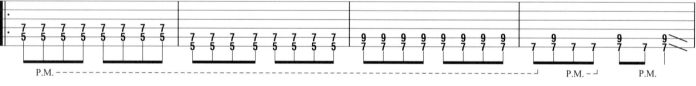

end - less. Bring it on home Oh,
o - pen, bring it all home. 'Cause

Gtr. 2

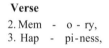

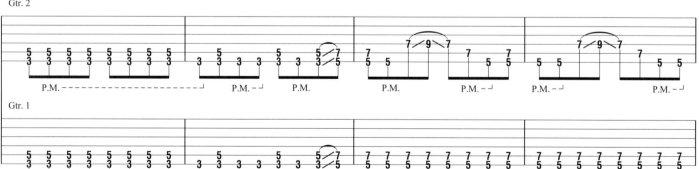

Gtr. 1

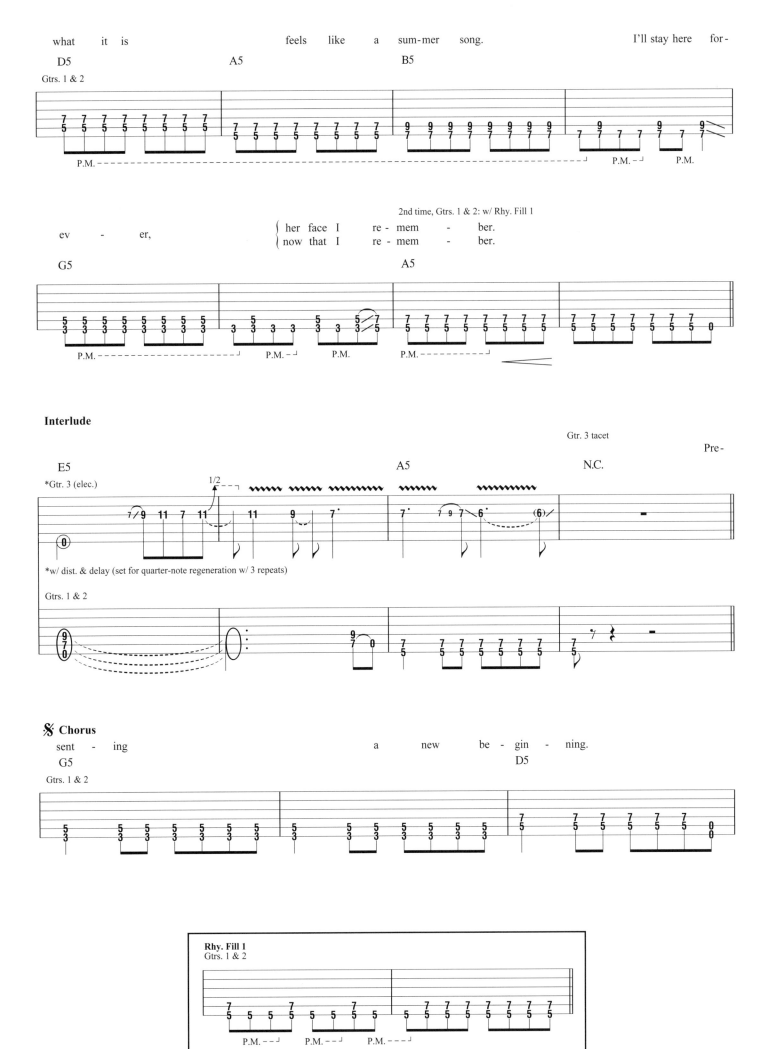

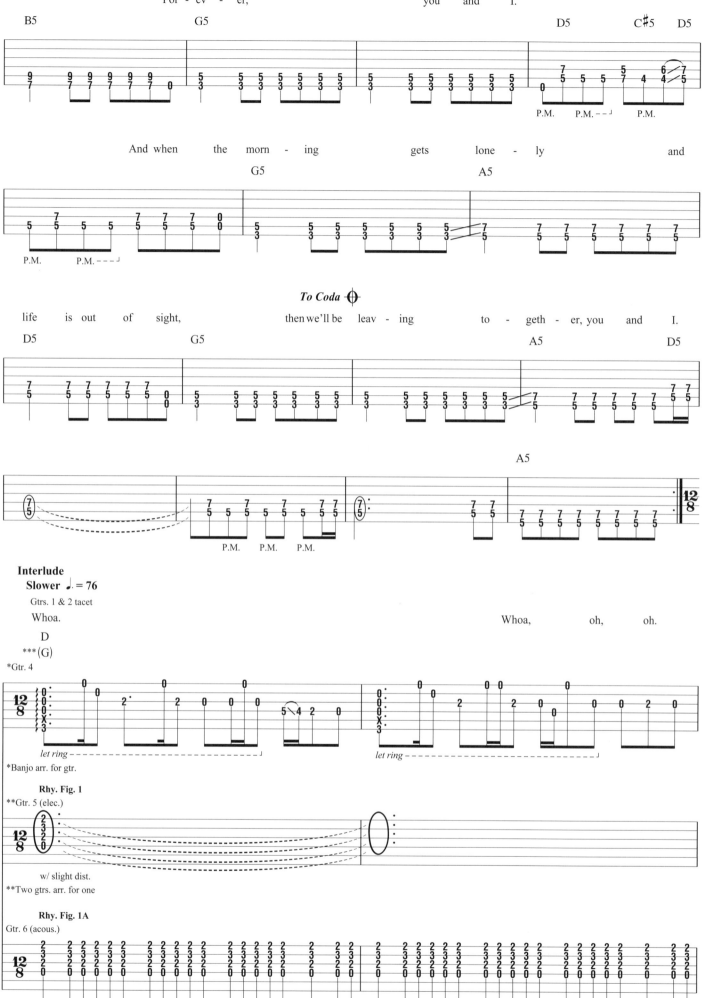

For - ev - er, you and I.

And when the morn - ing gets lone - ly and

To Coda ⊕

life is out of sight, then we'll be leav - ing to - geth - er, you and I.

Interlude
Slower ♩. = 76

Gtrs. 1 & 2 tacet
Whoa. Whoa, oh, oh.

D
***(G)
*Gtr. 4

let ring - - - - - - -
let ring - - - - - - - - - - - - - -

*Banjo arr. for gtr.

Rhy. Fig. 1
**Gtr. 5 (elec.)

w/ slight dist.
**Two gtrs. arr. for one

Rhy. Fig. 1A
Gtr. 6 (acous.)

***Symbols in parentheses represent chord names respective to capoed guitar.
Symbols above reflect actual sounding chord. Capoed fret is "0" in tab.
Chord symbols reflect basic harmony.

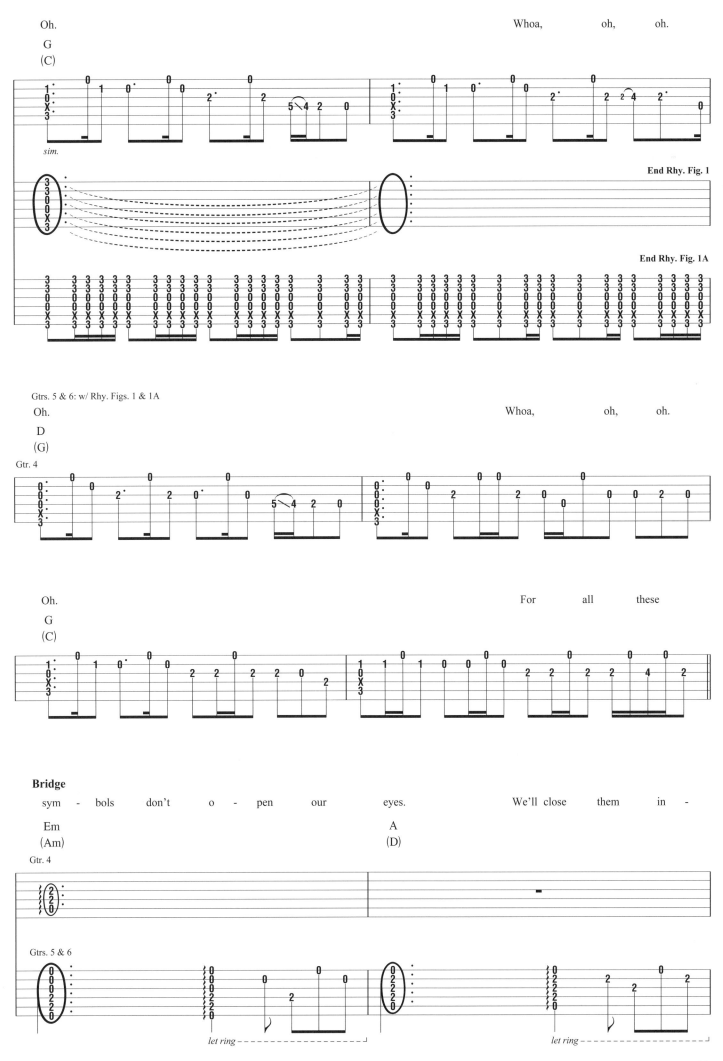

stead,　　　leave the mes - sen-ger　　be - hind.　　　　　　But one　day　we will

D　　　　　　　　　　Dsus4　D　　　　　　G
(G)　　　　　　　　　(Gsus4) (G)　　　　　(C)

Gtr. 4

Gtr. 5

Gtr. 6

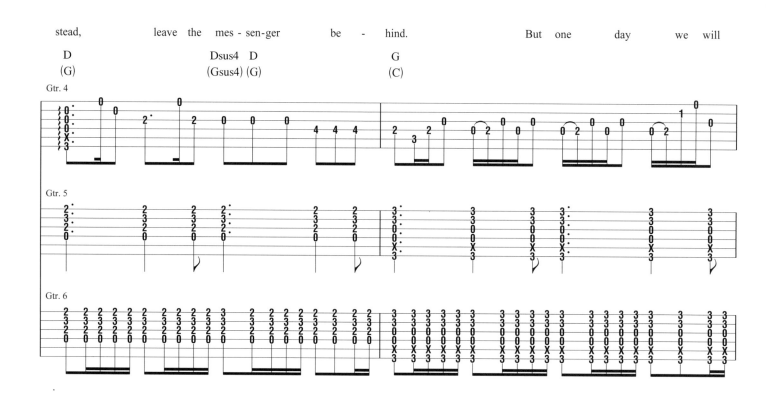

Free time

know.　　　　　　　　　　　　　　　　　　　　　　　　　　　　Pre -

A
(D)

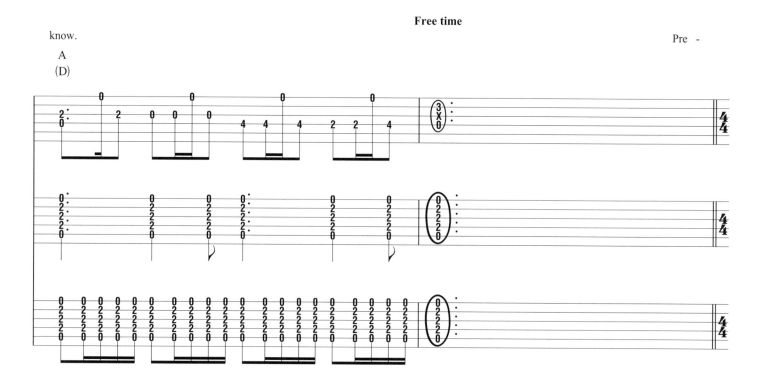

Chorus
A tempo

Gtrs. 4, 5 & 6 tacet

sent - ing　　　　　　　　　a　new　beg - in - ing.　　　　For-

G5　　　　　　　　　　　　　　　D5　　　　　　　　　　B5

Gtr. 1

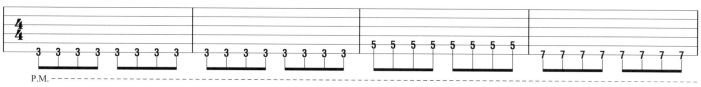

P.M. -

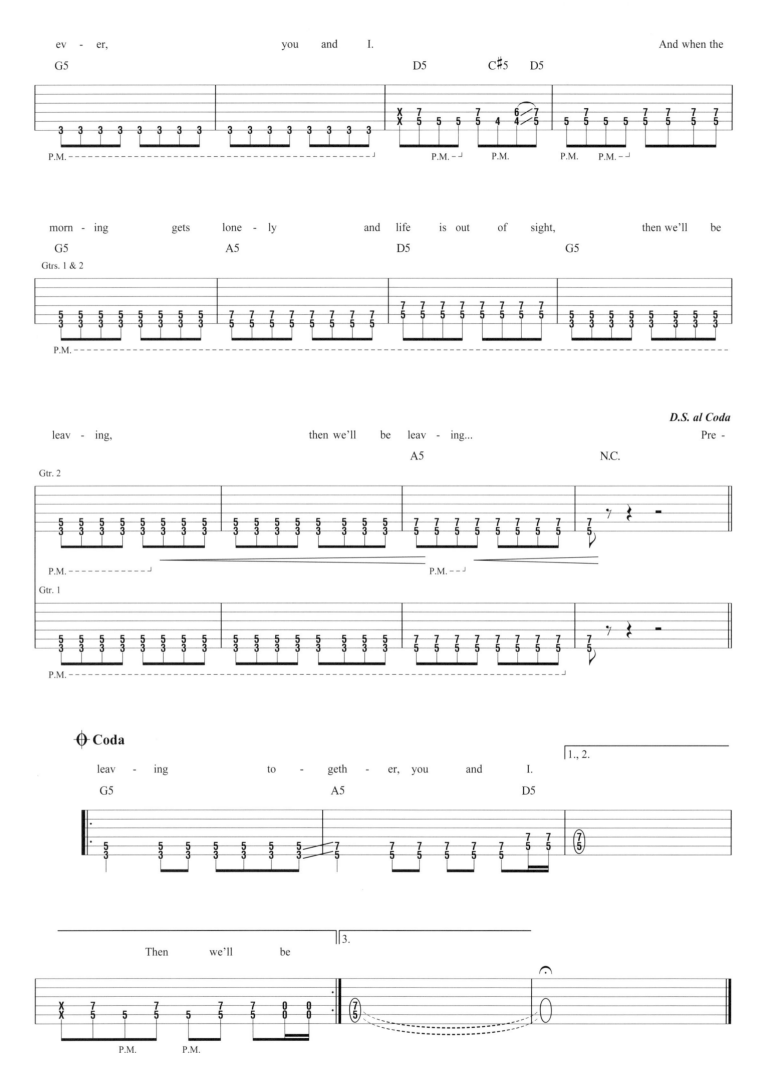

The Gates of Babylon

Words and Music by Michael Poulsen, Jon Larsen and Rob Caggiano

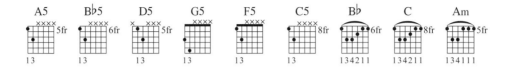

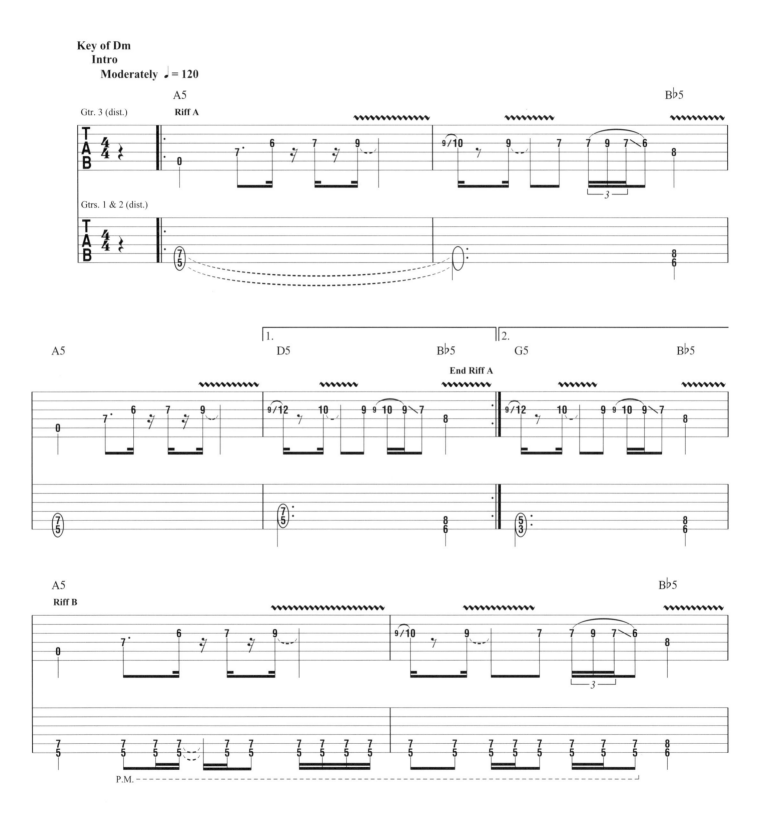

A5   G5   Bb5

End Riff B

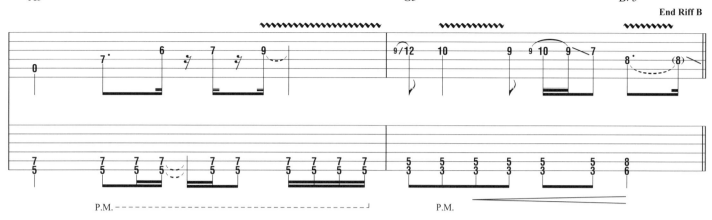

P.M.

Verse

Gtr. 3 tacet

wak - en - ing   a   god - dess in the   dark,   on   a
2. Sent   by   Lord   En - ki to   find   the   god - dess

A5

Gtrs. 1 & 2

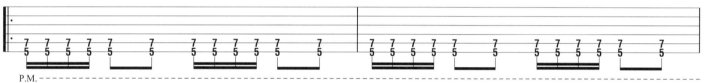

P.M.

2nd time, Gtr. 4: w/ Fill 1

stake,   she's   been   hang - ing like a   doll.   Tried   to
Ish   -   tar   and   bring her back   to   life.   The   tale   of

Bb5

*Gtr. 4

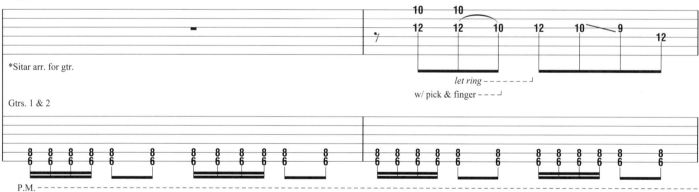

*Sitar arr. for gtr.

let ring

w/ pick & finger

Gtrs. 1 & 2

P.M.

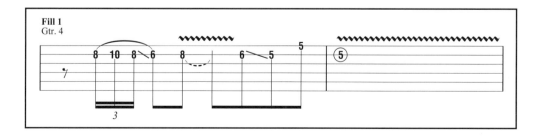

Fill 1
Gtr. 4

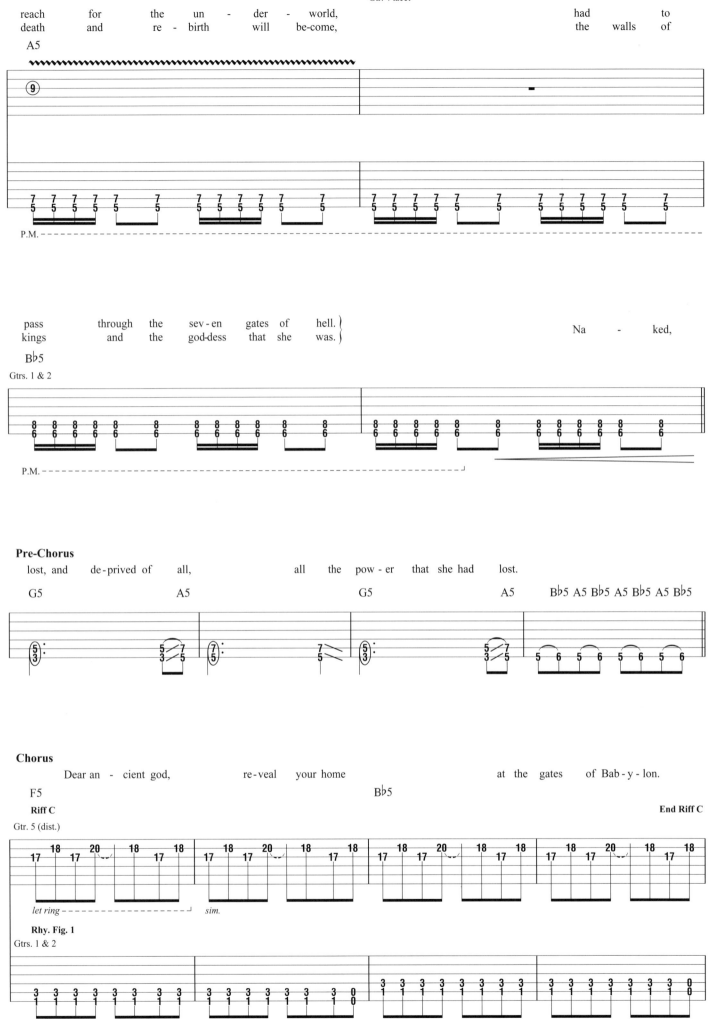

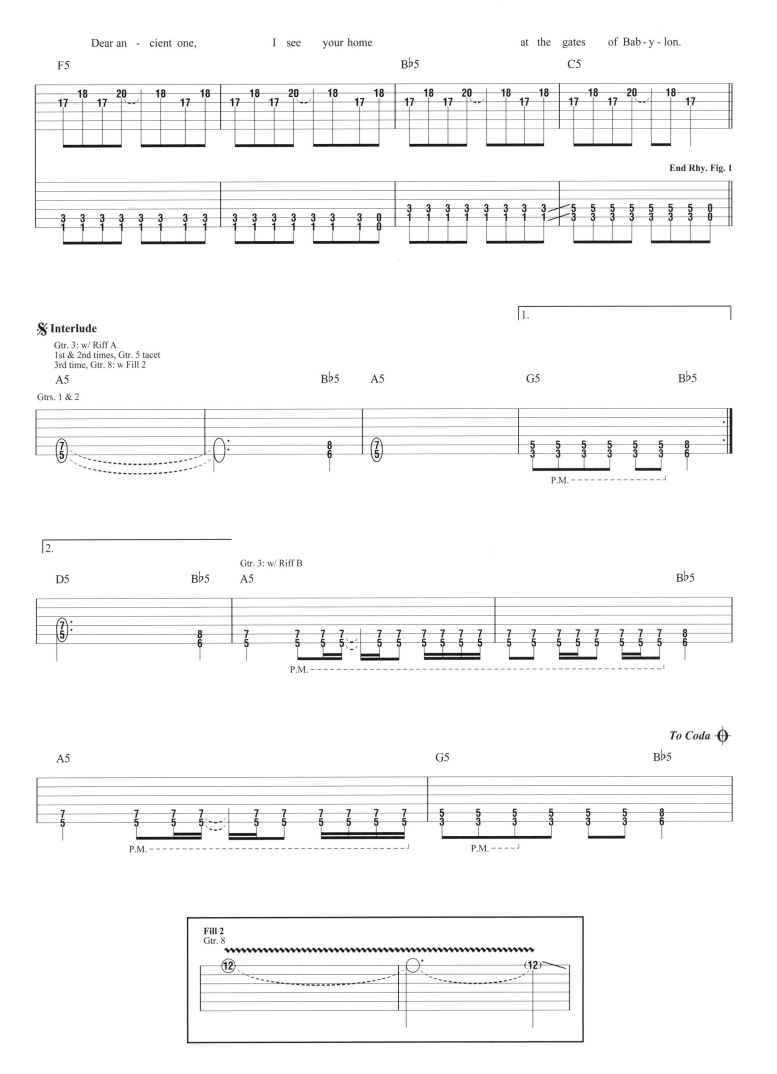

N.C.

Gtr. 2

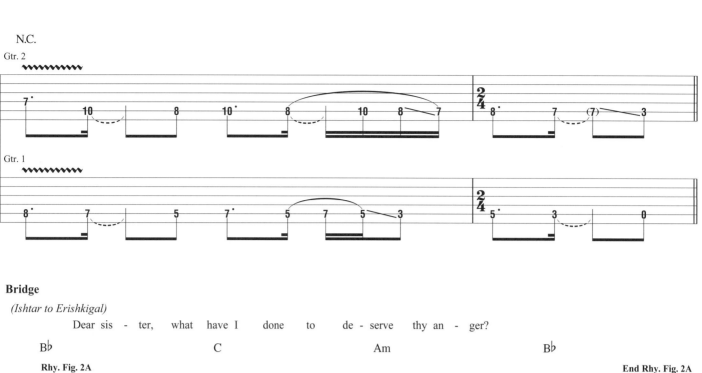

Gtr. 1

Bridge

(Ishtar to Erishkigal)

Dear sis - ter, what have I done to de - serve thy an - ger?

Bb   C   Am   Bb

Rhy. Fig. 2A   End Rhy. Fig. 2A

*Gtr. 6 (clean)

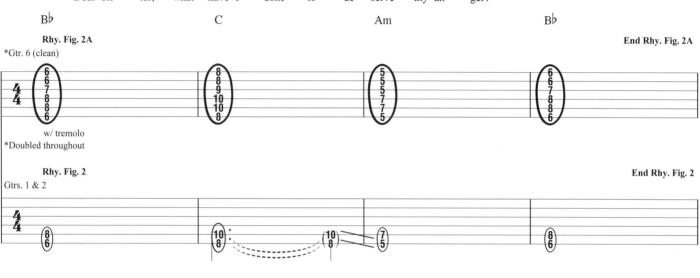

w/ tremolo
*Doubled throughout

Rhy. Fig. 2   End Rhy. Fig. 2
Gtrs. 1 & 2

Gtrs. 1 & 2: w/ Rhy. Fig. 2
Gtr. 6: w/ Rhy. Fig. 2A

I passed through the sev - en gates, now all I had is yours.

C   Am   Bb

Gtr. 7 (slight dist.)

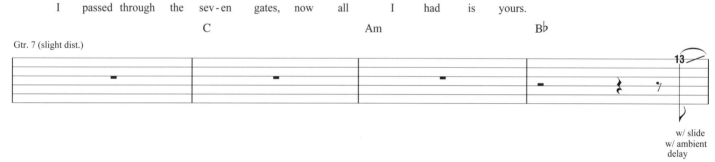

w/ slide
w/ ambient
delay

The un - der - world that you rule, I be - came a vic - tim of.

Bb5   C5   A5   Bb5

Gtr. 7

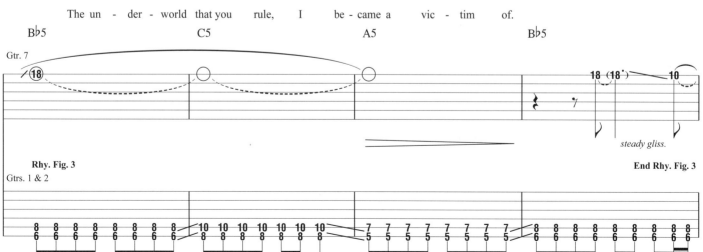

steady gliss.

Rhy. Fig. 3   End Rhy. Fig. 3
Gtrs. 1 & 2

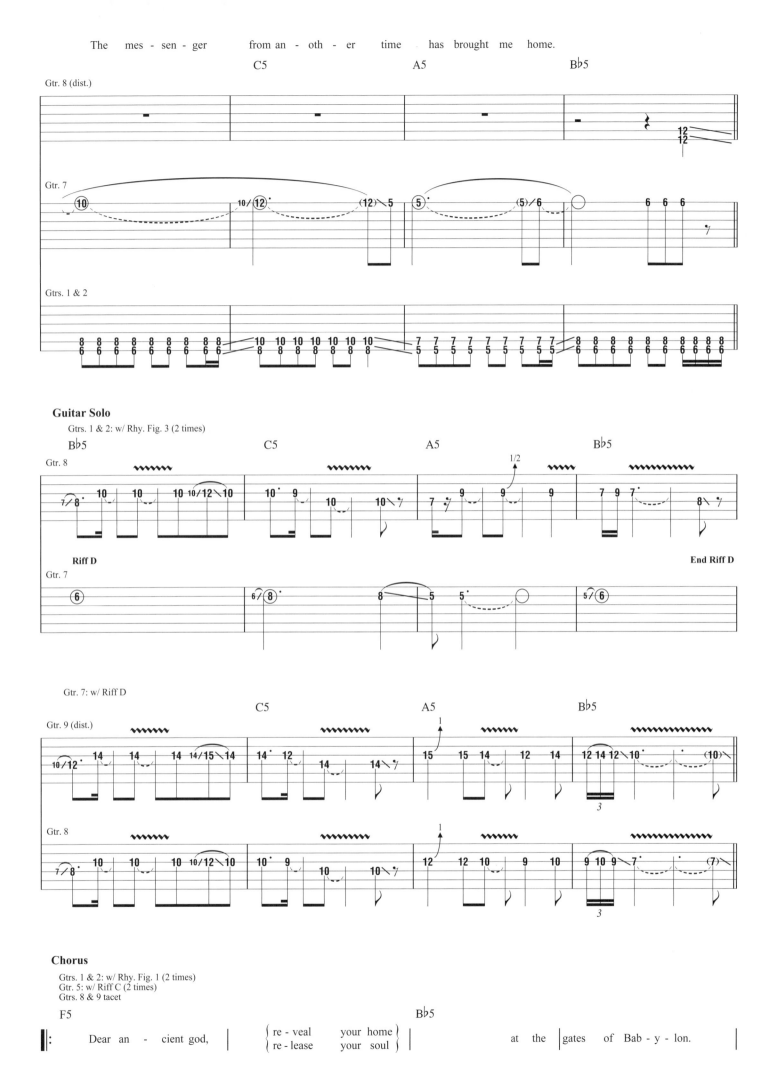

F5   Bb5   C5

Dear an - cient one,   I see your home   at the gates of Bab - y - lon.

Interlude

Gtrs. 1 & 2: w/ Rhy. Fig. 1
Gtr. 5: w/ Riff C (2 times)

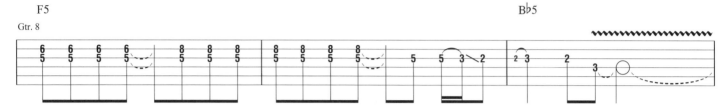

At the

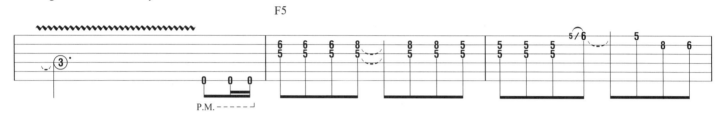

gates of Bab - y - lon.

D.S. al Coda
(take 2nd ending)

At the gates of Bab - y - lon.

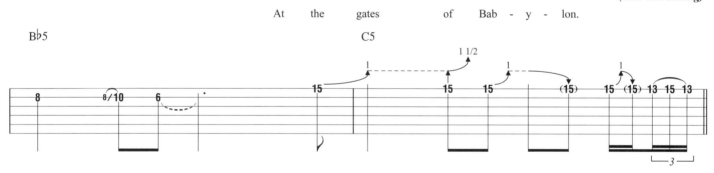

⊕ Coda

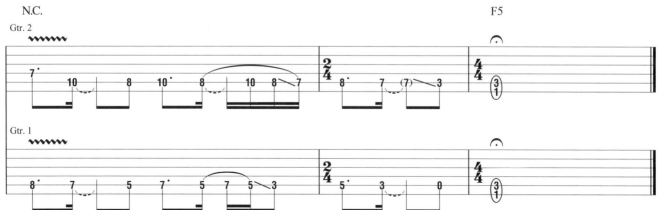

Let It Burn

Words and Music by Michael Poulsen

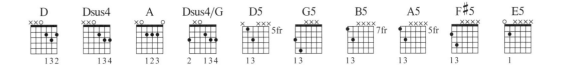

Key of D
Intro
Moderately ♩ = 108

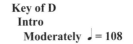

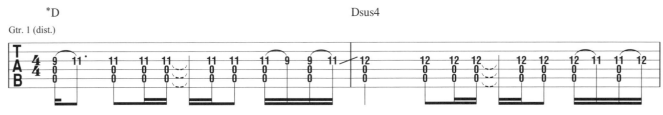

*Chord symbols reflect basic harmony.

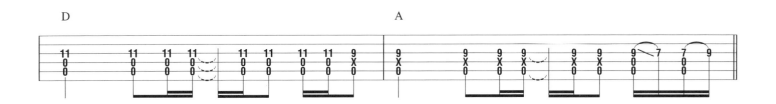

Chorus

Tell the lone - ly   where to go.

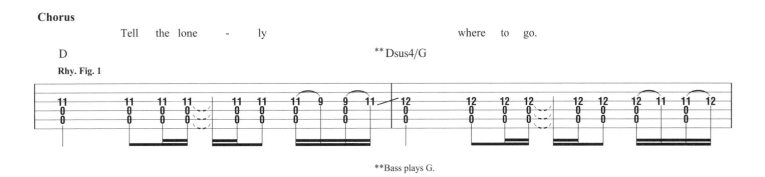

**Bass plays G.

Kill the in - side   and let it burn.

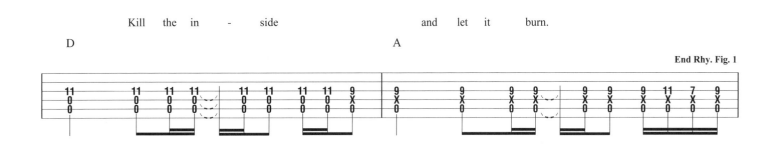

D   Dsus4/G   D   A

He's not the on - ly   with - out hope.   Kill the in - side   and let it burn.

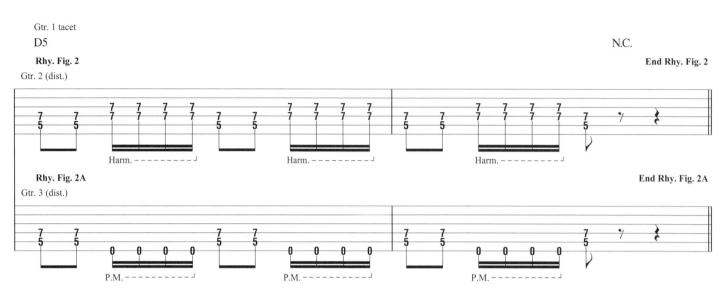

Verse

2nd time, Gtr. 5 tacet

1. The   fi - re may   not   o -   pen, but the   Dev - il   will re - turn.

2. The   emp - ty eyes are   fall -   ing down the   path   of no   re - turn.

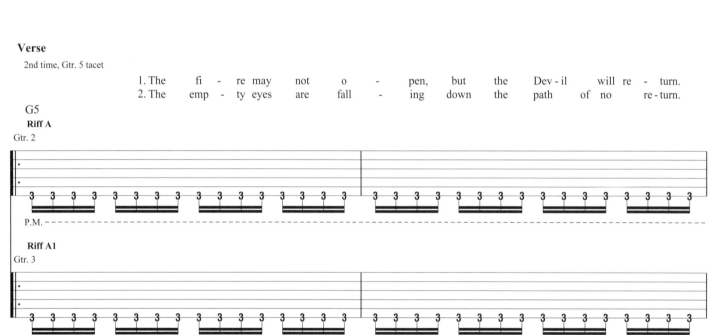

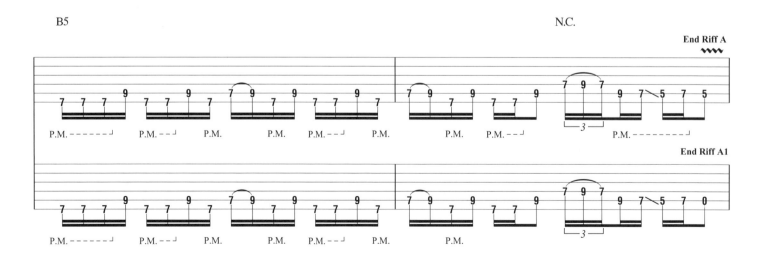

G5   B5   N.C.

In - san - i - ty   or glo │ - ry in a mind that nev-er learns. ⎱
In blind - ness   he wan │ - ders, if his mind will ev-er learn. ⎰

A mo-ment of some - thing where the dark can re-verse.

A5   B5   G5   A5   N.C.

Gtrs. 2 & 3

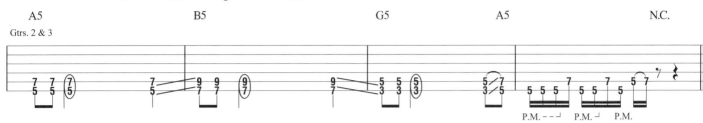

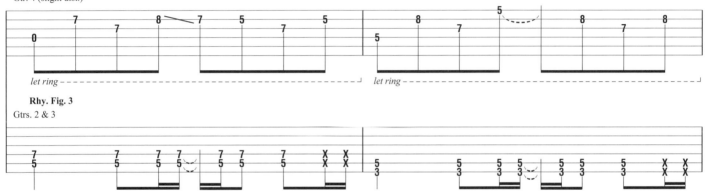

𝄋 Chorus

2nd time, Gtr. 6: w/ Fill 1

Tell   the lone - ly   where   to go.

D5   G5

Riff B
Gtr. 4 (slight dist.)

Rhy. Fig. 3
Gtrs. 2 & 3

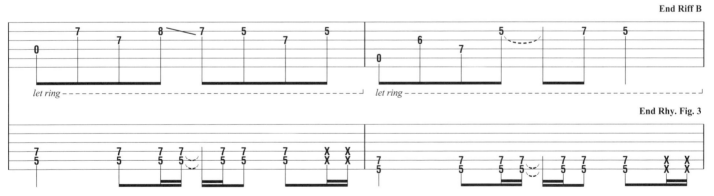

Kill   the in - side   and   let it   burn.

D5   A5

                                                                    End Riff B

let ring   let ring

                                                                    End Rhy. Fig. 3

Fill 1
Gtr. 6

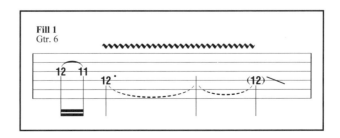

1st & 2nd times, Gtrs. 2 & 3: w/ Rhy. Fig. 3
1st & 2nd times, Gtr. 4: w/ Riff B
3rd time, Gtrs. 2 & 3: w/ Rhy. Fig. 3 (1st 3 meas.)
3rd time, Gtr. 4: w/ Riff B (1st 3 meas.)

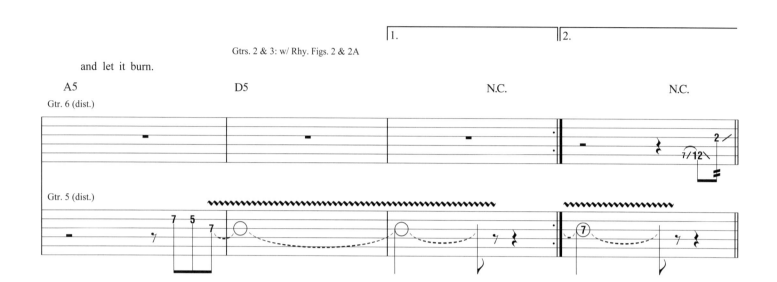

He's not the on - ly   with - out hope.   Kill the in - side

Gtrs. 2 & 3: w/ Rhy. Figs. 2 & 2A

and let it burn.

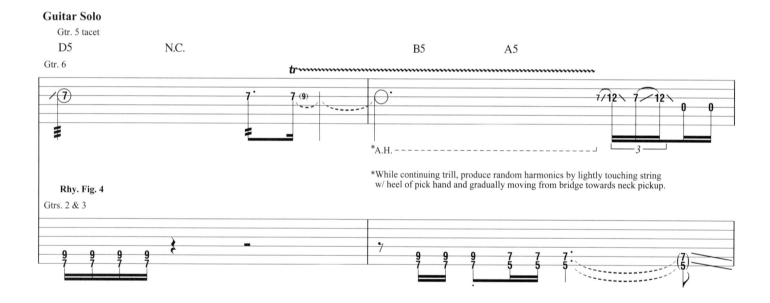

Guitar Solo

Gtr. 5 tacet

*While continuing trill, produce random harmonics by lightly touching string
w/ heel of pick hand and gradually moving from bridge towards neck pickup.

Rhy. Fig. 4

Gtrs. 2 & 3

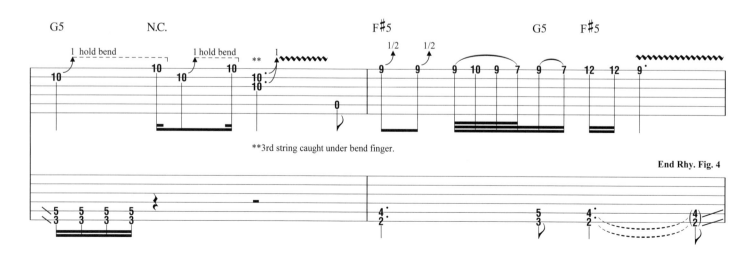

**3rd string caught under bend finger.

End Rhy. Fig. 4

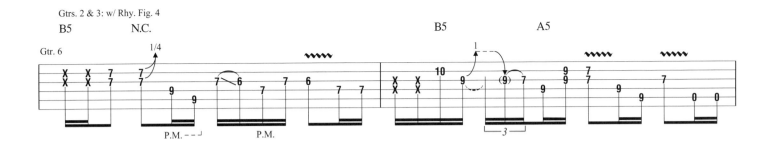

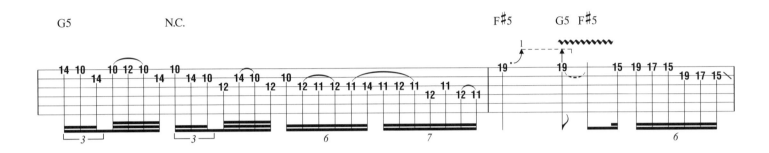

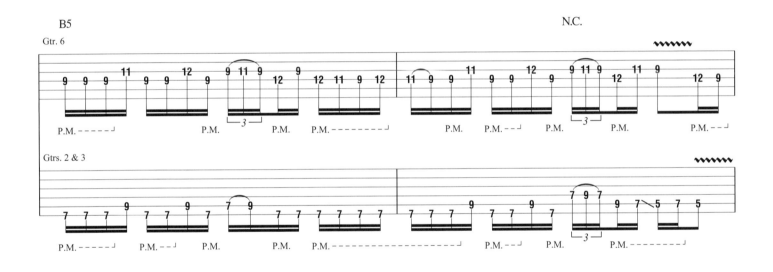

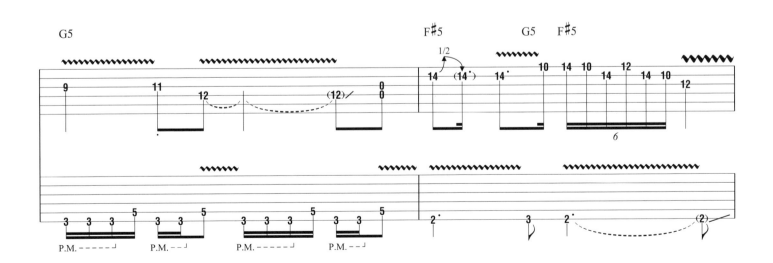

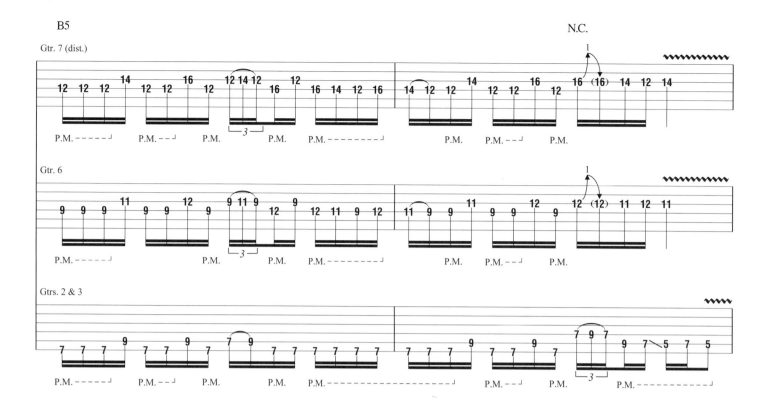

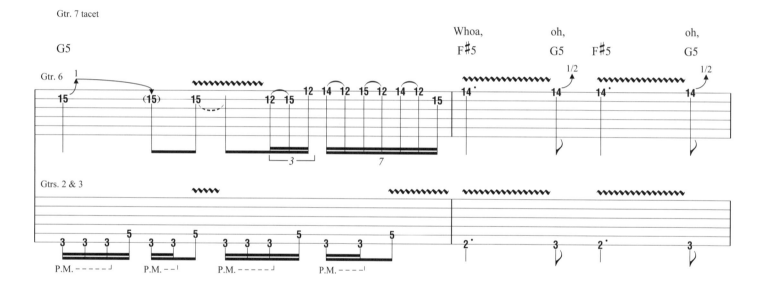

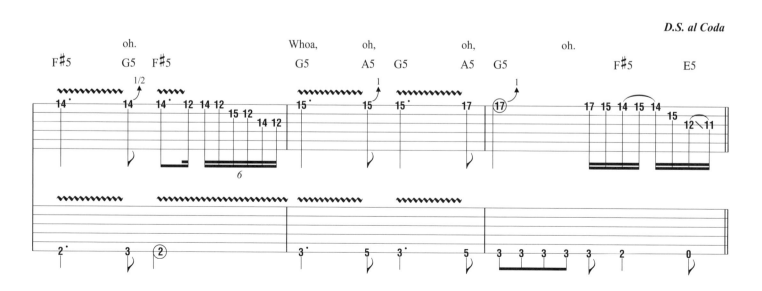

⊕ Coda

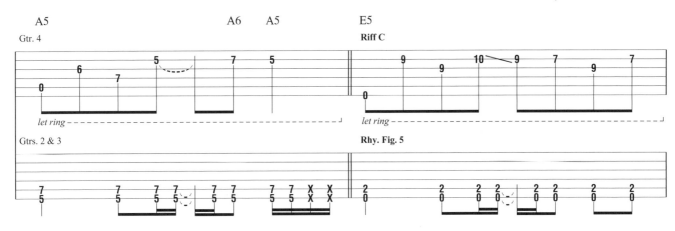

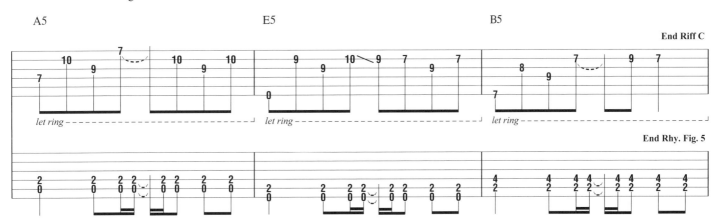

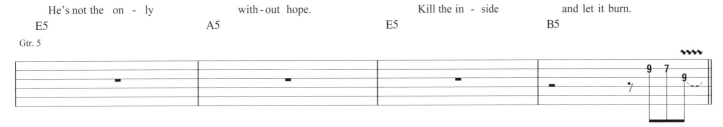

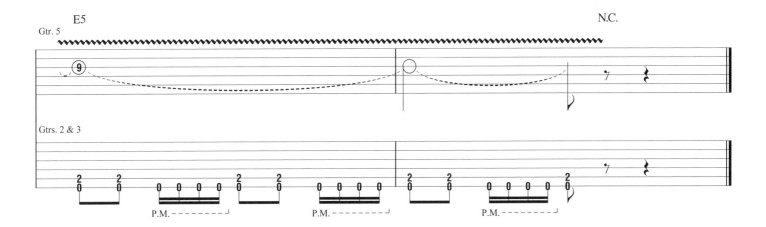

Black Rose

Words and Music by Michael Poulsen

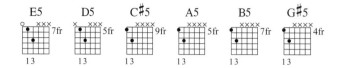

Key of E
Intro
Fast ♩ = 168

Count-ing days   'til it's   o - ver, my   friends, 'til it's   o - ver, my   friends, count a - long.

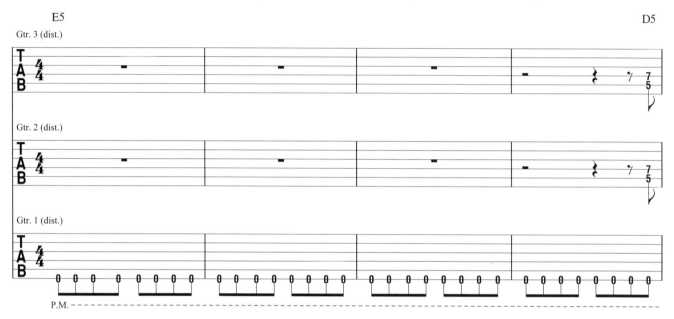

Gtr. 3 tacet

Count-ing days   'til it's   o - ver, my   friends,   o - ver, my   friends, count a - long.

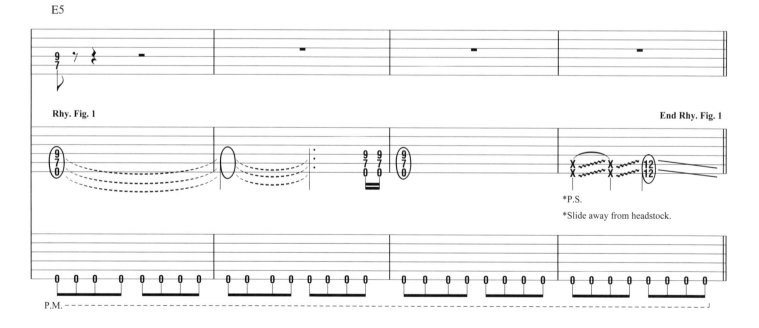

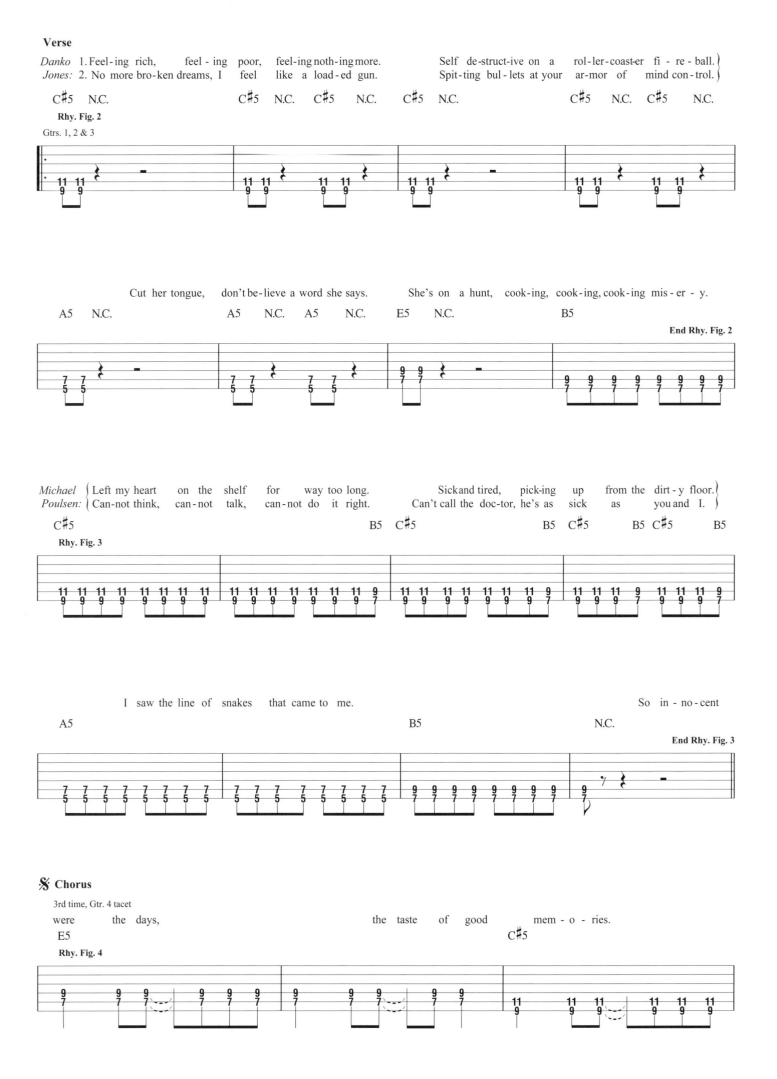

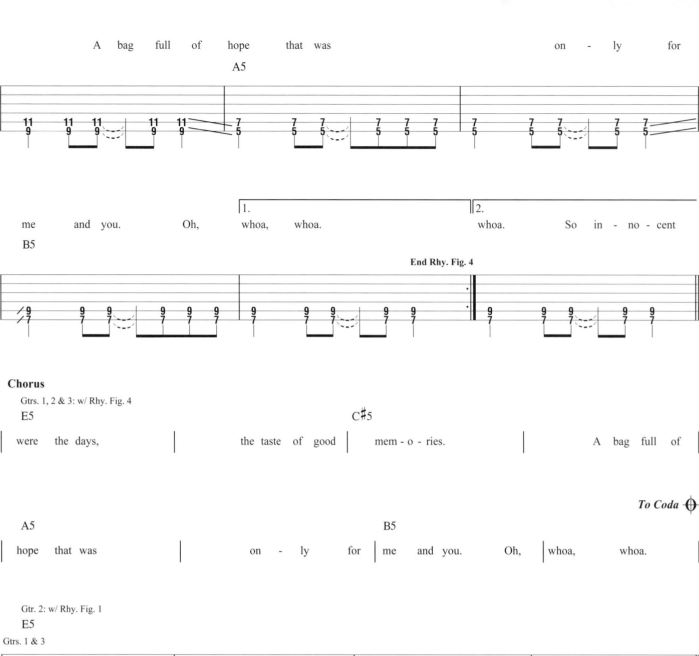

Chorus

Gtrs. 1, 2 & 3: w/ Rhy. Fig. 4

Gtr. 2: w/ Rhy. Fig. 1

Gtrs. 1 & 3

Interlude

Gtr. 3 tacet

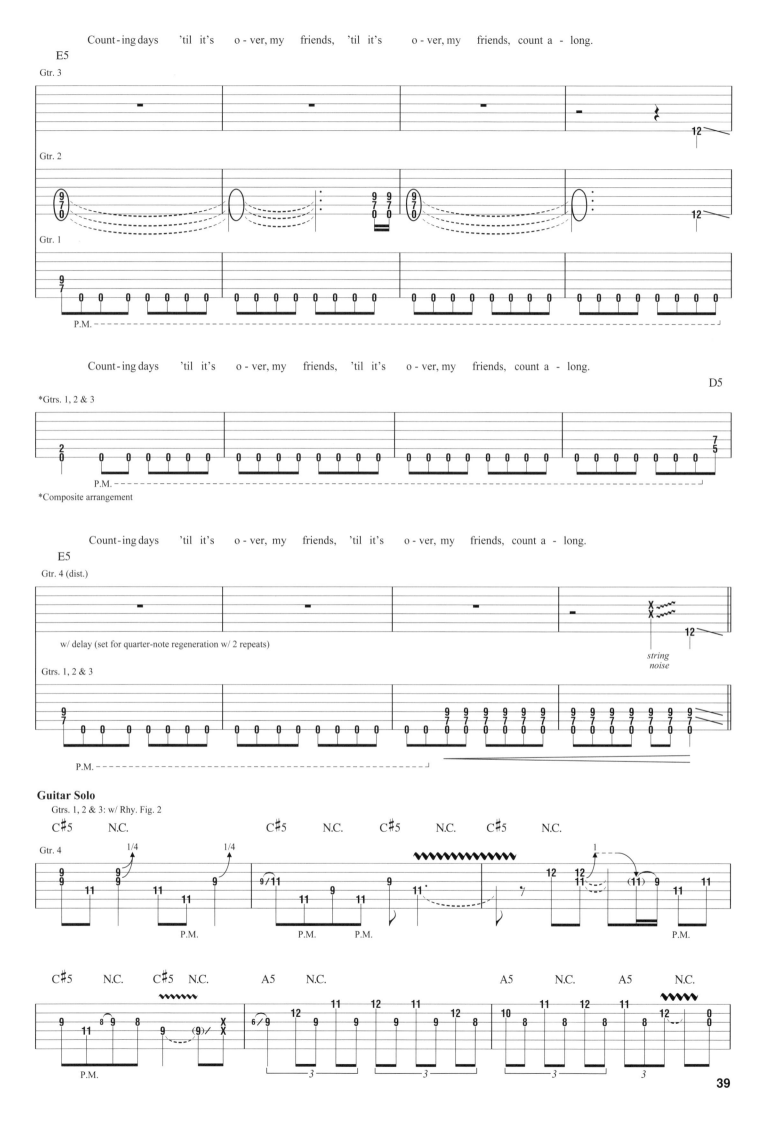

Count-ing days 'til it's o - ver, my friends, 'til it's o - ver, my friends, count a - long.

Count-ing days 'til it's o - ver, my friends, 'til it's o - ver, my friends, count a - long.

*Composite arrangement

Count-ing days 'til it's o - ver, my friends, 'til it's o - ver, my friends, count a - long.

w/ delay (set for quarter-note regeneration w/ 2 repeats)

string
noise

Guitar Solo

Gtrs. 1, 2 & 3: w/ Rhy. Fig. 2

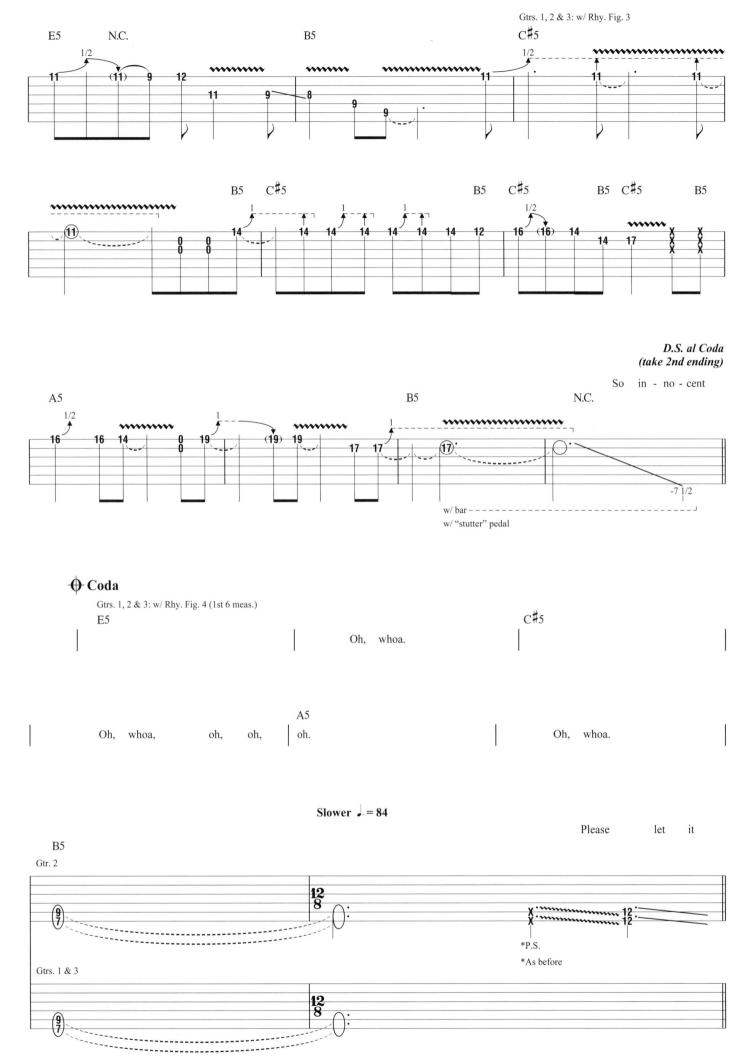

Outro

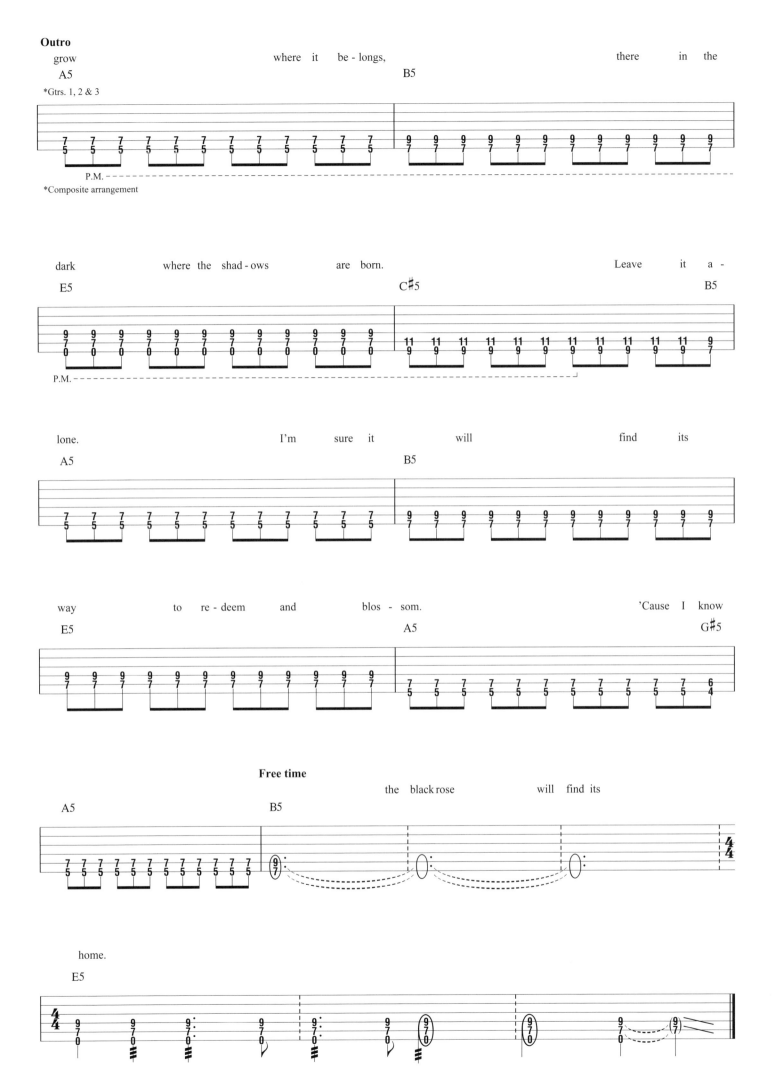

Rebound

Words and Music by Ray Carlisle

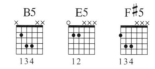

Key of B
Intro
Moderately fast ♩ = 144

N.C.

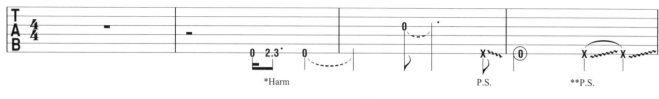

*Harm

P.S.   **P.S.

*Harmonic located one-third the
distance between 2nd & 3rd frets.

**Slide away from
headstock.

B5

Gtrs. 1 & 2 (dist.)

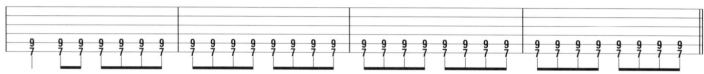

Verse

1., 2. It's a shame   that you don't know   me   'cause I   nev-er made it past   the third   { string.
{ string, no,   no.

B5   E5   F#5
Rhy. Fig. 1   **End Rhy. Fig. 1**

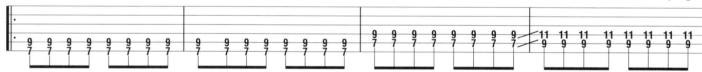

Gtrs. 1 & 2: w/ Rhy. Fig. 1 (3 times)

B5   E5   F#5

My coach nev-er | gave me a chance, he's al-ways | blow-ing his whis-tle at | me.

B5   E5   F#5

Put me in your game   and I | prom-ise not   to shoot a | three, I'll stick with | twos.   I don't

B5   E5   F#5

wan-na make a steal un-less you | make a   pass. I'll | nev-er per-son-al foul | you.   Did you

Chorus

have to give your boy-friend all my let-ters? I did-n't

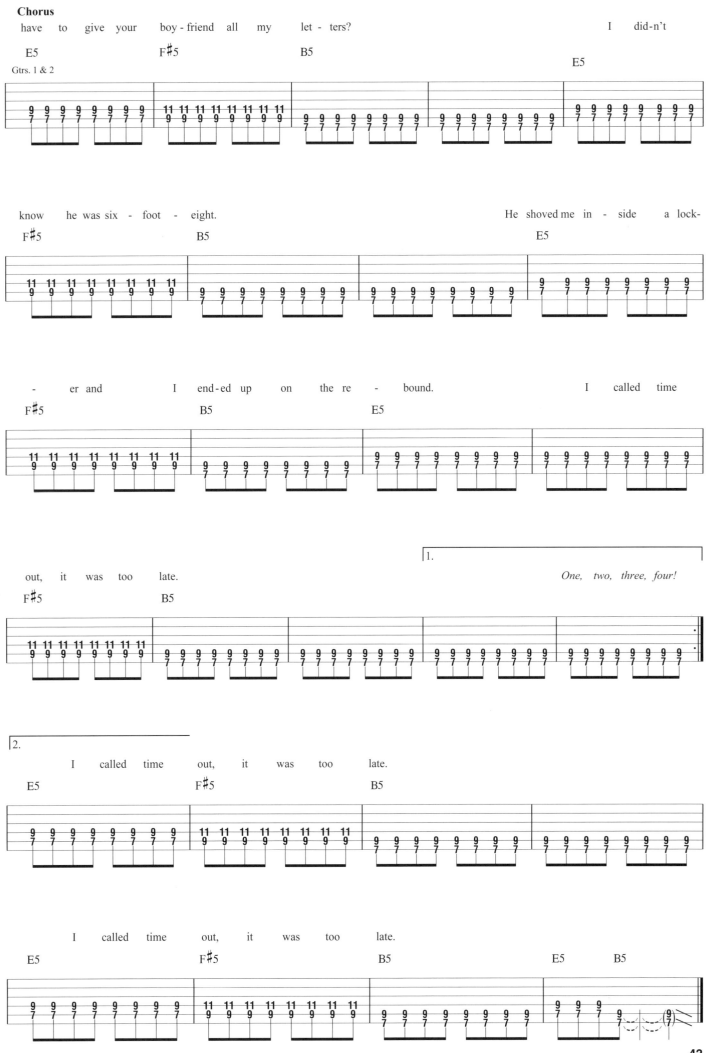

know he was six - foot - eight. He shoved me in - side a lock-

- er and I end-ed up on the re - bound. I called time

out, it was too late. *One, two, three, four!*

1.

2.

I called time out, it was too late.

I called time out, it was too late.

Mary Jane Kelly

Words and Music by Michael Poulsen

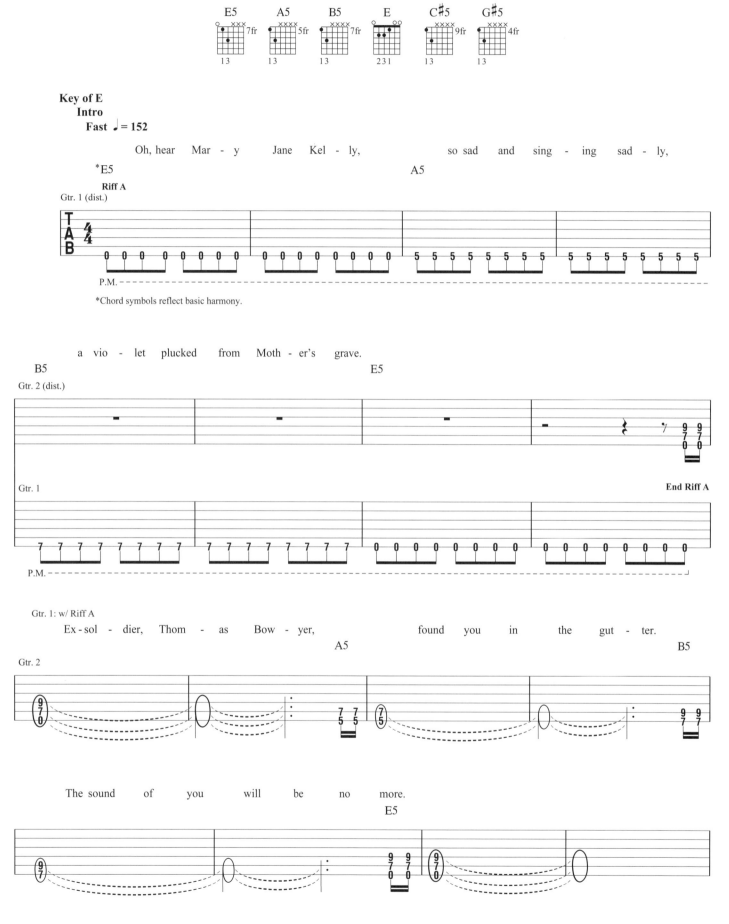

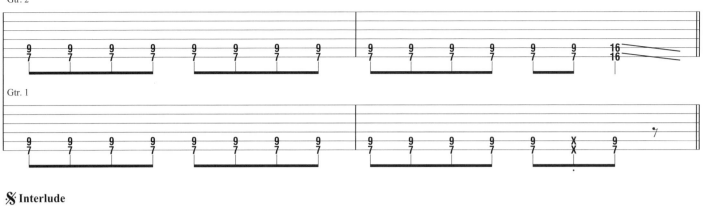

%% Interlude

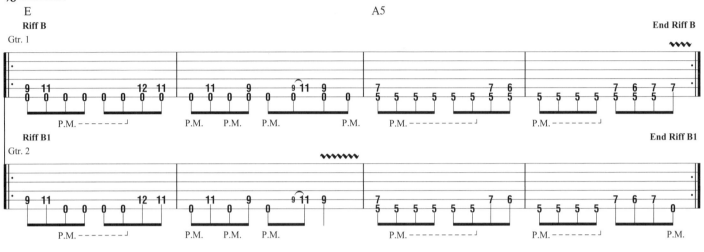

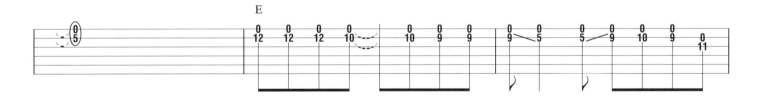

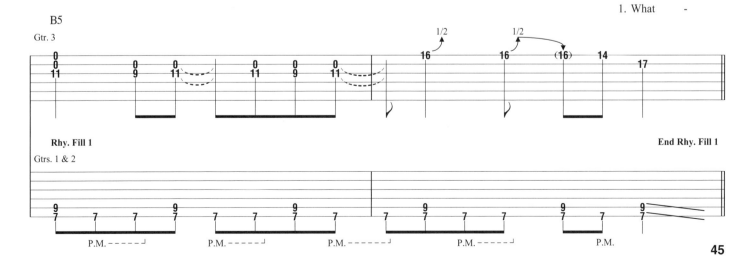

Verse

2nd time, Gtr. 3 tacet

1st time, Gtr. 3 tacet

ev - er you had said or ev - er done
Mar - y, wake up, let your spir - it rise.

won't
Who

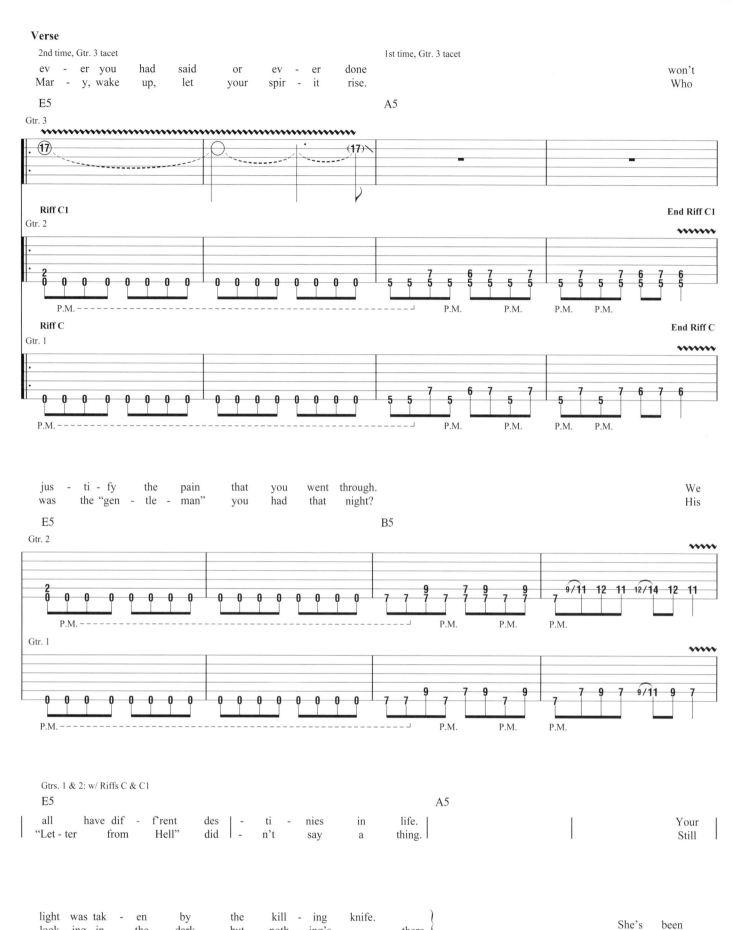

jus - ti - fy the pain that you went through.
was the "gen - tle - man" you had that night?

We
His

all have dif - f'rent des - ti - nies in life.
"Let - ter from Hell" did - n't say a thing.

Your
Still

light was tak - en by the kill - ing knife.
look - ing in the dark, but noth - ing's there.

She's been

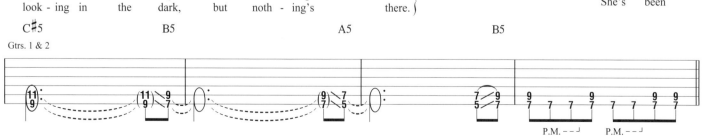

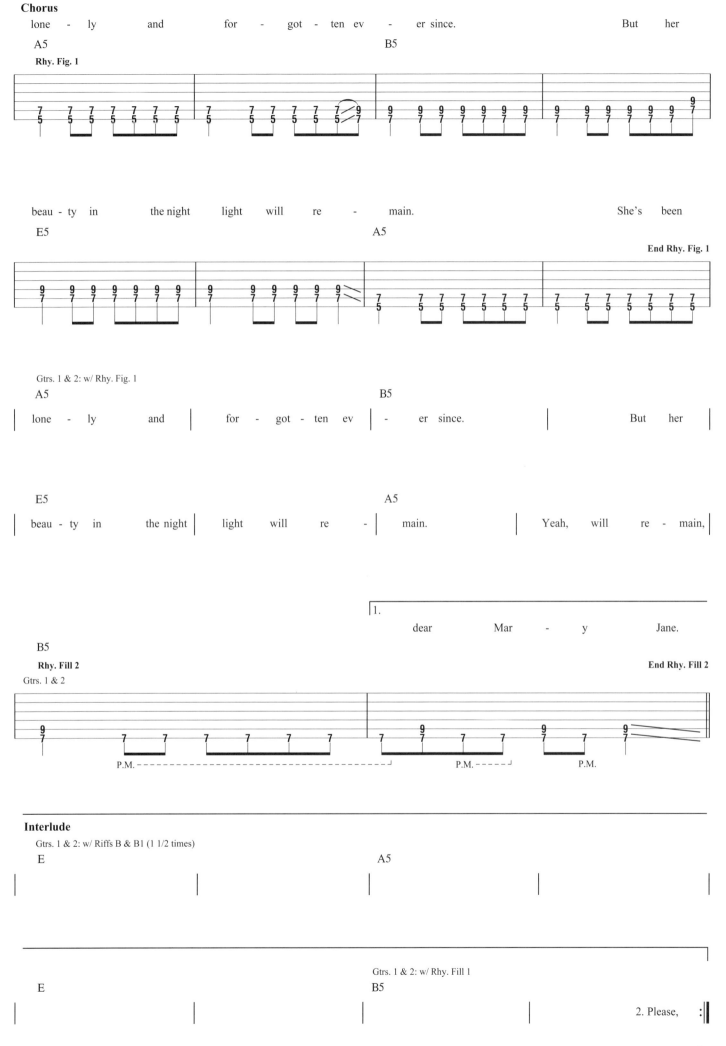

2.

Interlude
Half-time feel

dear   Mar -   y   Jane

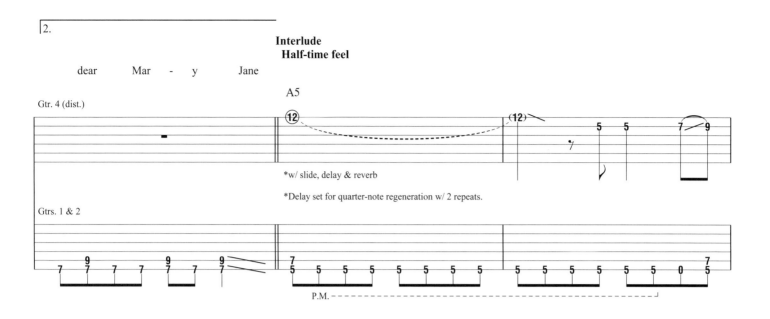

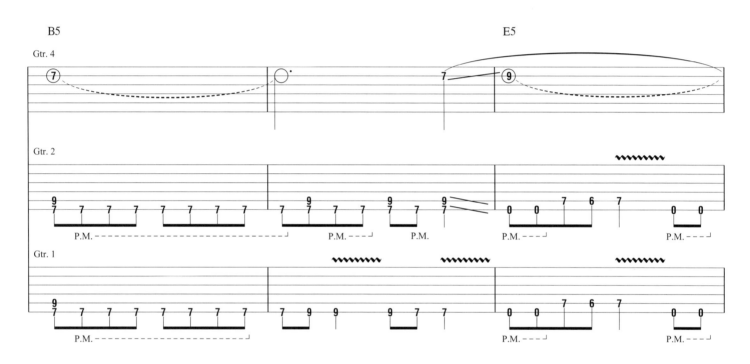

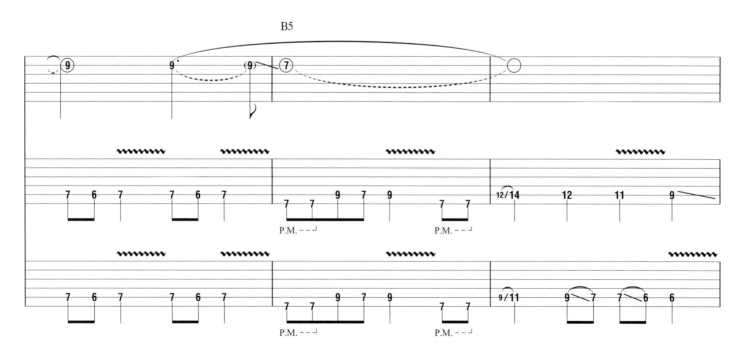

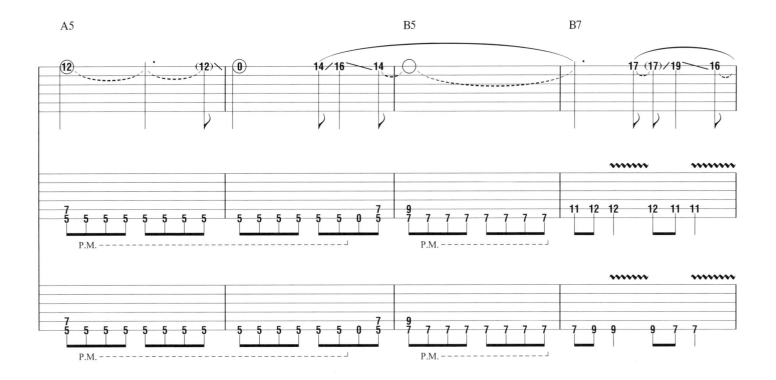

End half-time feel

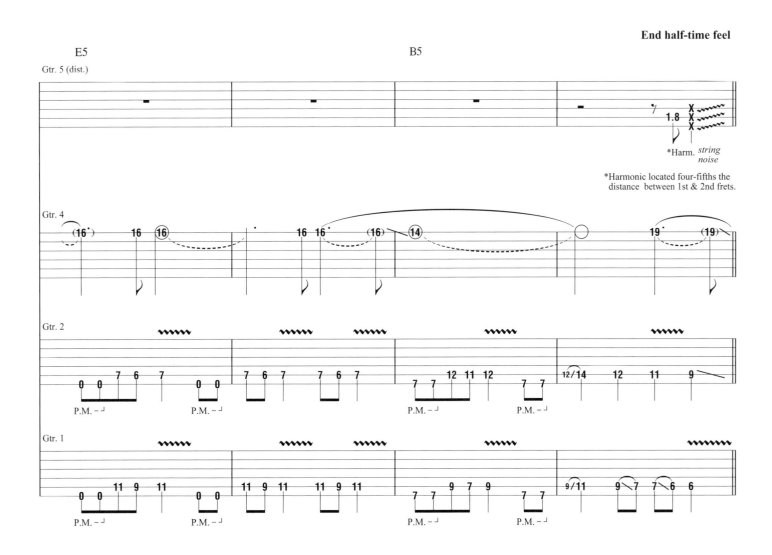

Guitar Solo

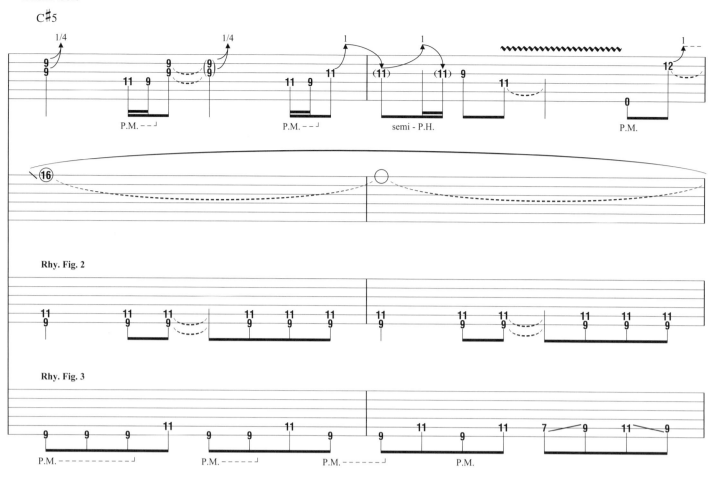

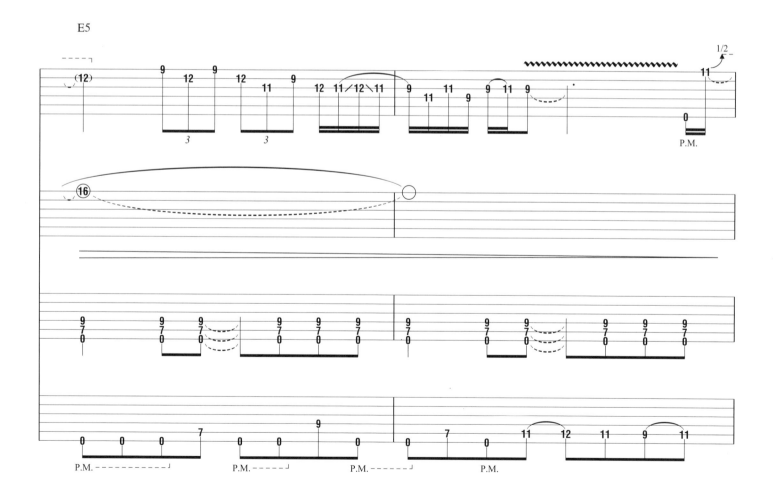

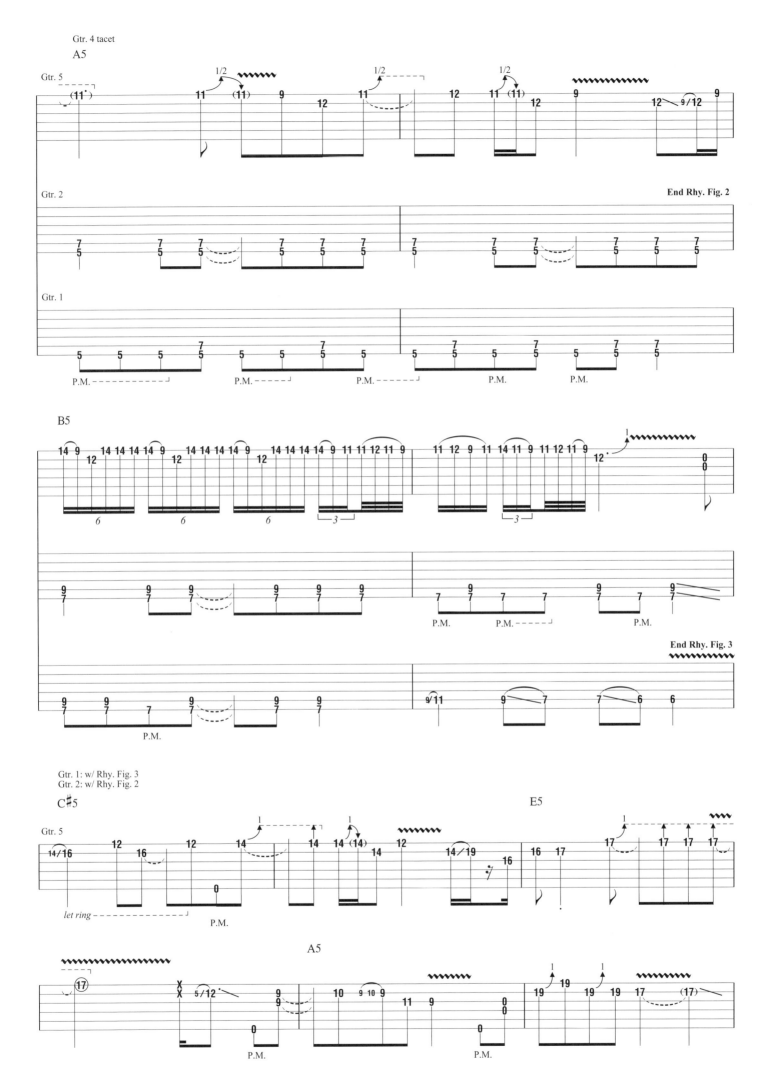

B5

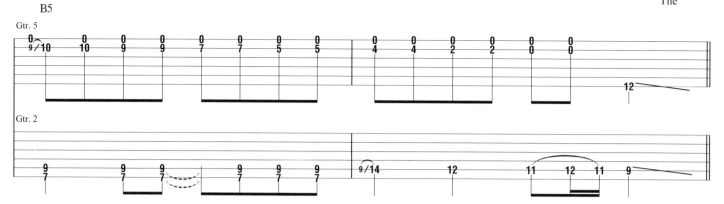

Bridge

Gtr. 5 tacet

nem - e - sis is ne - glect.   Run - ning on the wolves' path.   Try to get the blood - y facts.   Where do all the an - gels wait?

G#5   A5

Rhy. Fig. 4

Gtrs. 1 & 2

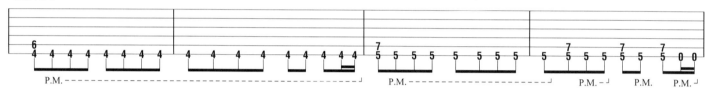

Let   it   be,   yeah, may - be   just   let   it   be.   A

E5   B5

End Rhy. Fig. 4

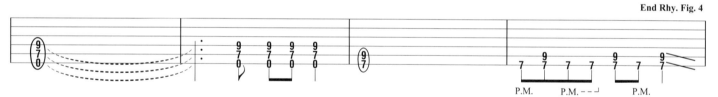

Gtrs. 1 & 2: w/ Rhy. Fig. 4

G#5

vio - let plucked from Moth - er's grave.   Do   the   sing - ing,   do   the   dance.

A5   E5

Show me, where's the ev - i - dence?   Where do   all   the vic - tims lay? Or   let   it   be,

B5

yeah, may - be   just   let   it   be.   She's   been

Chorus

lone - ly   and   for - got - ten ev -   er since.   But her

A5   B5

Gtrs. 1 & 2

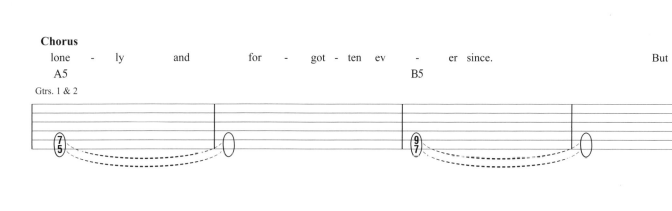

Gtrs. 1 & 2: w/ Rhy. Fig. 1 (last 4 meas.)

E5   A5

beau - ty   in   the night   light   will   re -   main.   She's been

Gtrs. 1 & 2: w/ Rhy. Fig. 1

                                             B5

lone - ly   and   for - got - ten ev   -   er since.   But her

E5   A5

beau - ty   in   the night   light   will   re -   main.

D.S. al Coda
(take repeat)

Gtrs. 1 & 2: w/ Rhy. Fill 2

B5

    Yeah,   will   re - main,   dear   Mar -   y   Jane.

⊕ Coda

Free time

E5

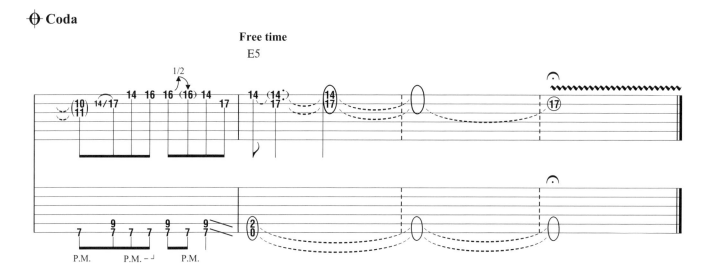

Goodbye Forever

Words and Music by Michael Poulsen

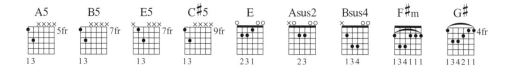

Tune down 1 step:
(low to high) D-G-C-F-A-D

Key of E
 Intro
  Moderately ♩ = 116

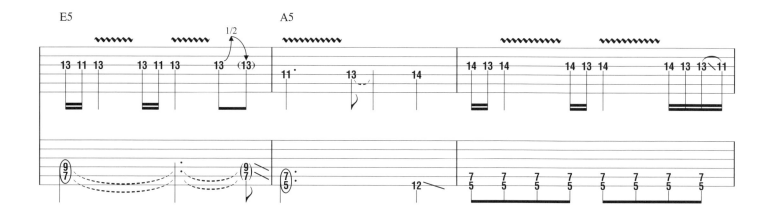

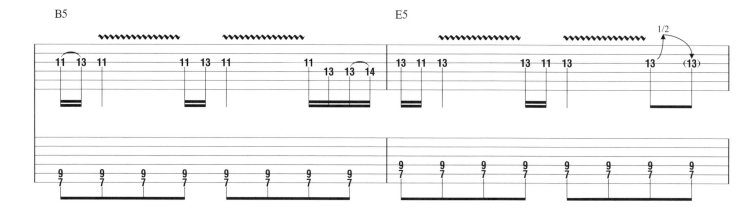

C#5 B5

End Riff A

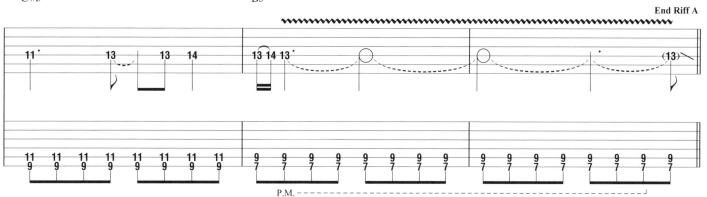

𝄋 Verse

Gtrs. 1, 2 & 3 tacet

1. Did you say   the thing you   want - ed?   Have you ev - er   felt   in
2. Were you lis-ten-ing to the   eve - ning?   Have you ev - er   felt   the dawn?

E

Rhy. Fig. 1

*Gtr. 4 (acous.)

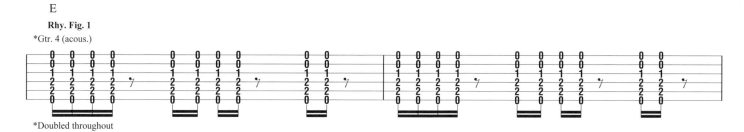

*Doubled throughout

love?   A mo - ment where no   prob - lems   would   ev - er   get you   down.
When   ev - 'ry - thing a - round   you   told   sto - ries   from the   world.

Asus2

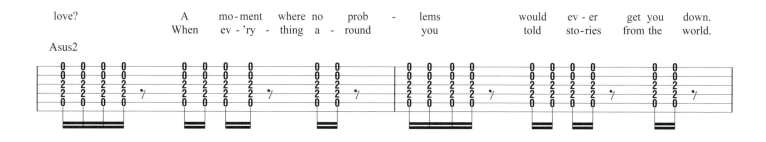

Free   as an ea - gle   but   on - ly   for   a
Dear   Moth - er Na - ture   speaks   loud - er   than   you

Bsus4   Asus2

Riff B

Gtr. 5 (elec.)

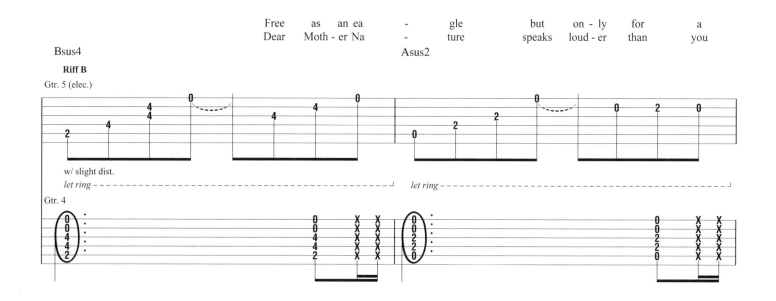

w/ slight dist.

let ring -   *let ring* -

Gtr. 4

55

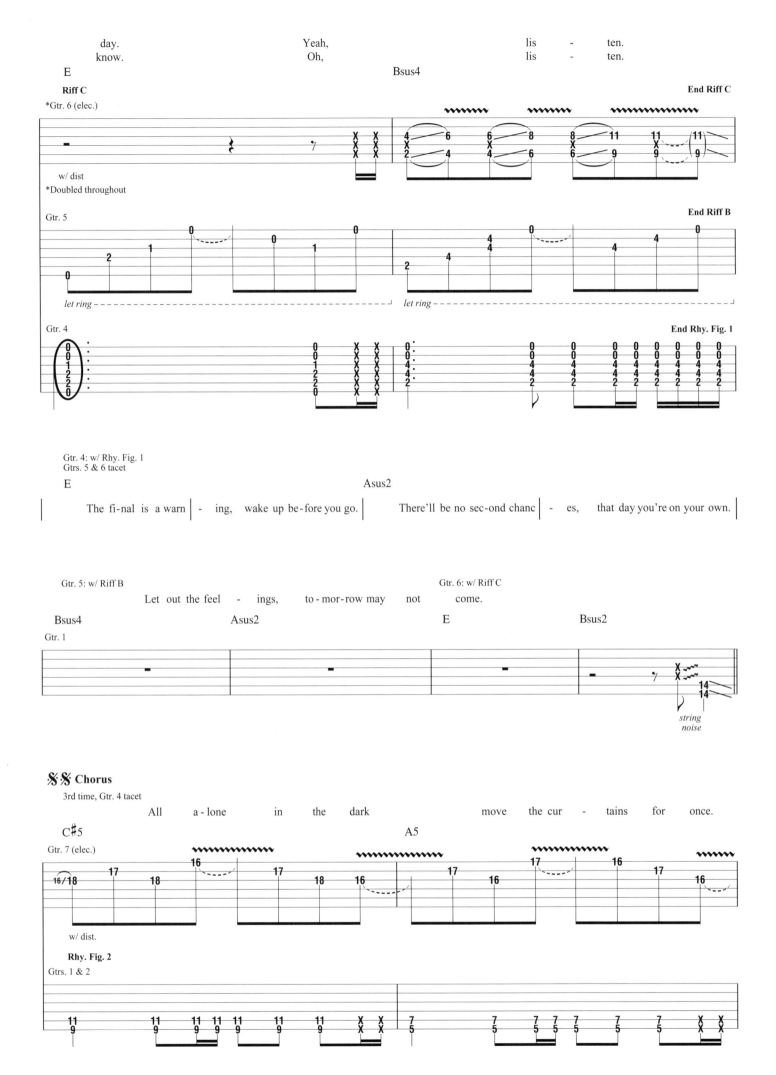

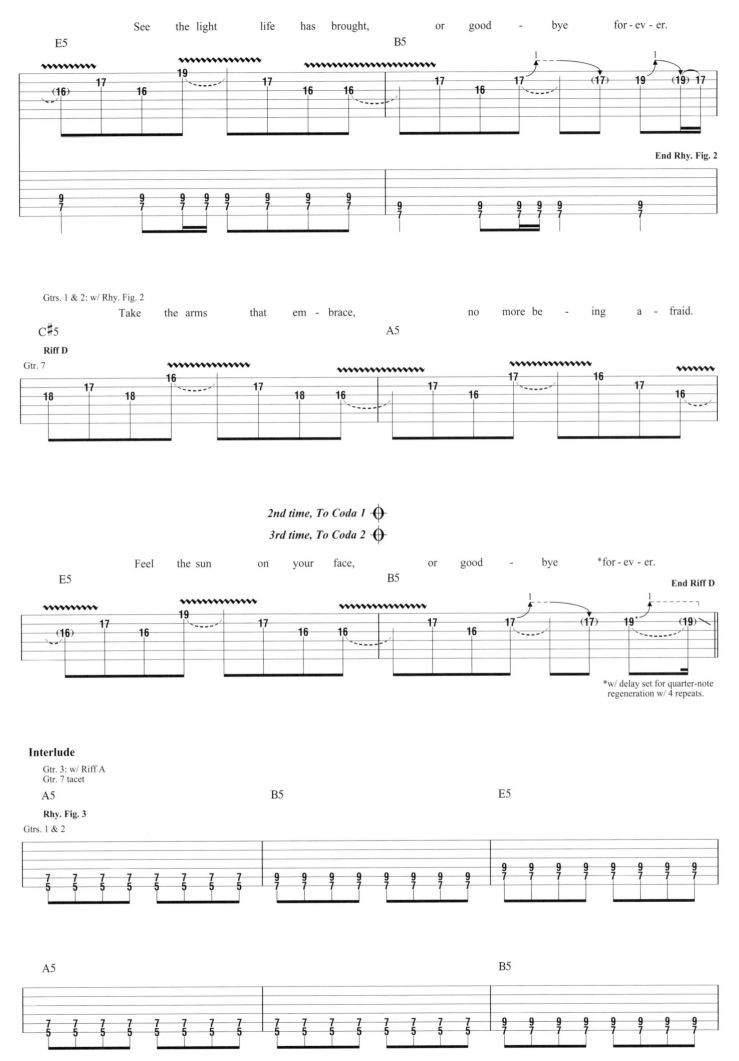

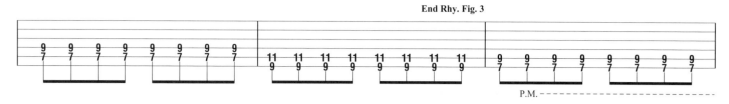

⊕ Coda 1

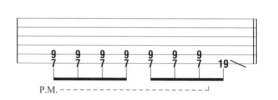

D.S. al Coda 1

or good - bye for-ev - er.

Gtr 7 tacet

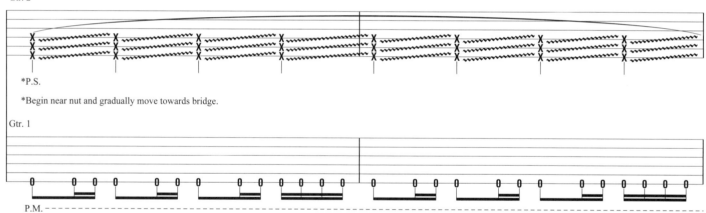

Interlude

E5

Gtr. 2

*P.S.

*Begin near nut and gradually move towards bridge.

Gtr. 1

P.M. -

We are the birth.

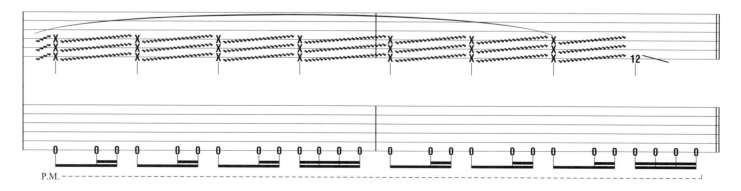

Bridge

We are the end.   We are the souls.

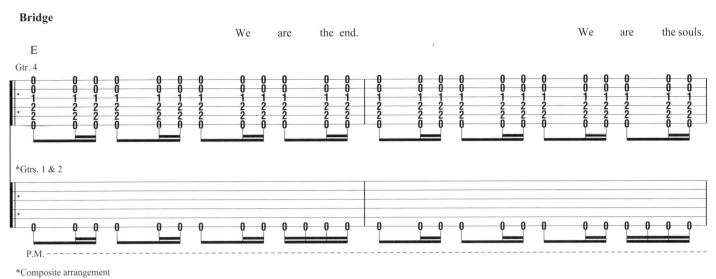

*Gtrs. 1 & 2

P.M. -

*Composite arrangement

We have a name.   We are the ris -

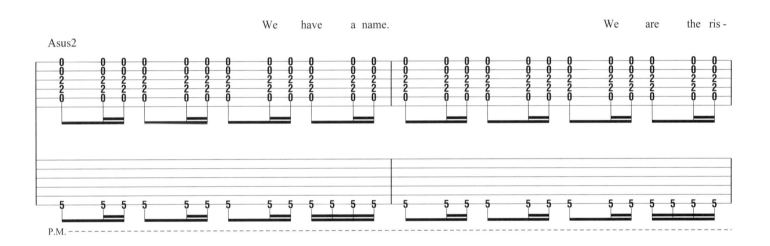

P.M. -

- ing and fall - ing ones.   We are the spir -

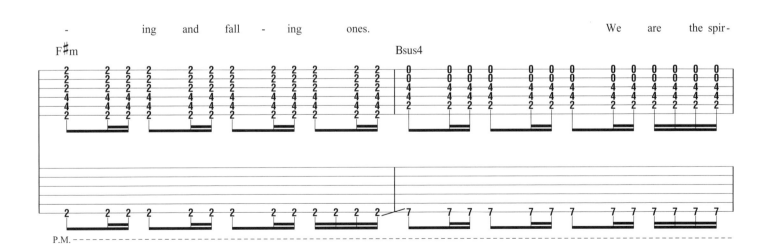

P.M. -

1.

- it for - ev - er more. (We are the birth.

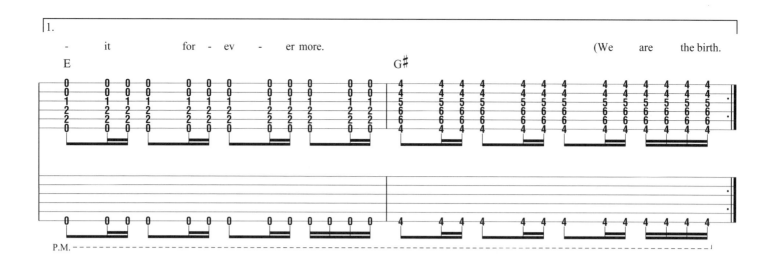

2.

D.S.S. al Coda 2

- it for - ev - er more.)

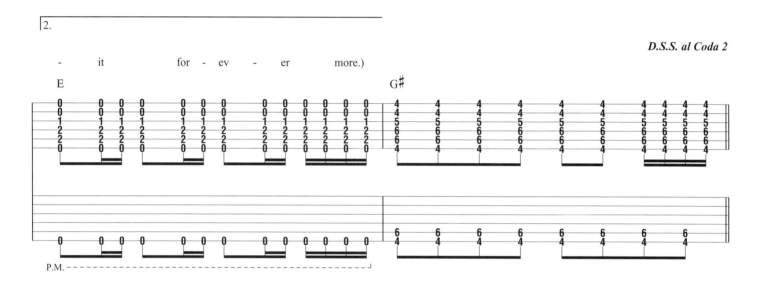

Coda 2

or good - bye for - ev - er.

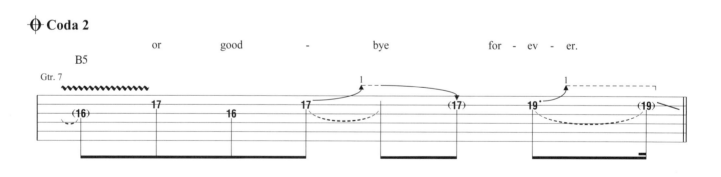

Chorus

Gtr. 7: w/ Riff D (2 times)

(All a - lone in the dark, pull the cur - tains for once.

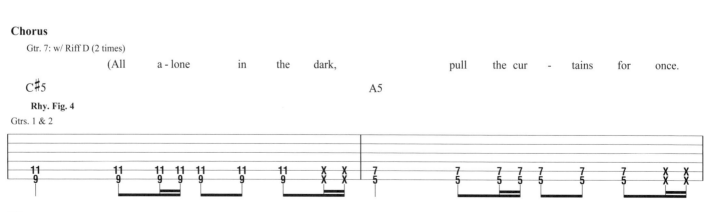

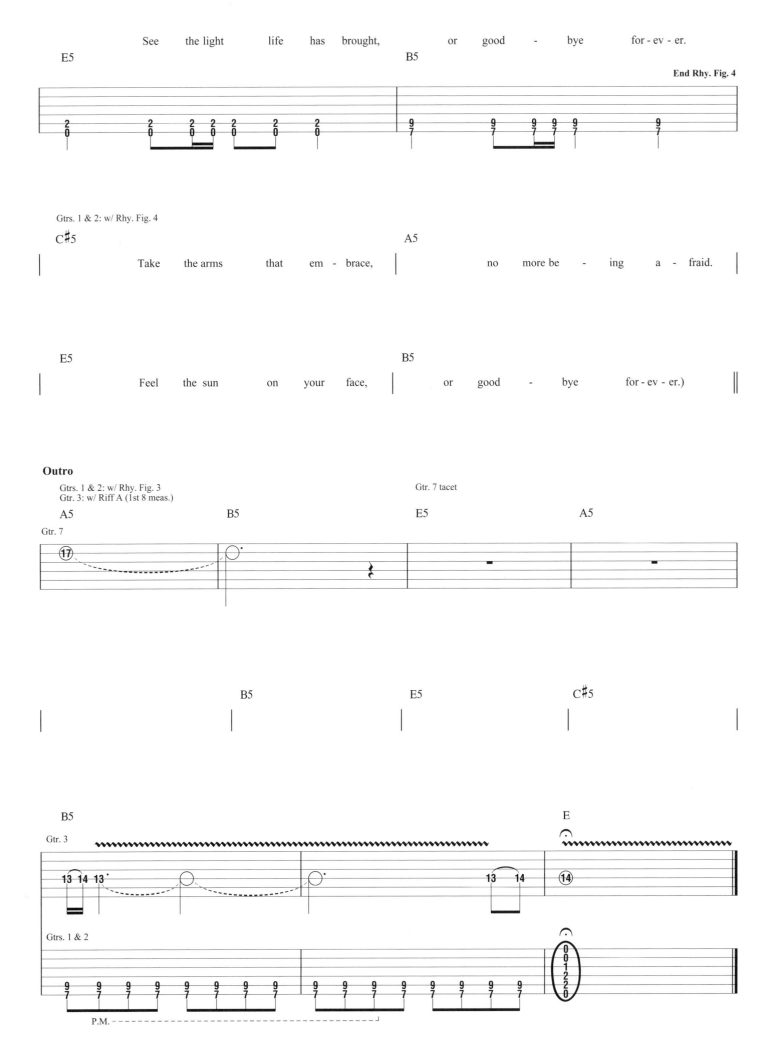

Seal the Deal

Words and Music by Michael Poulsen and Jon Larsen

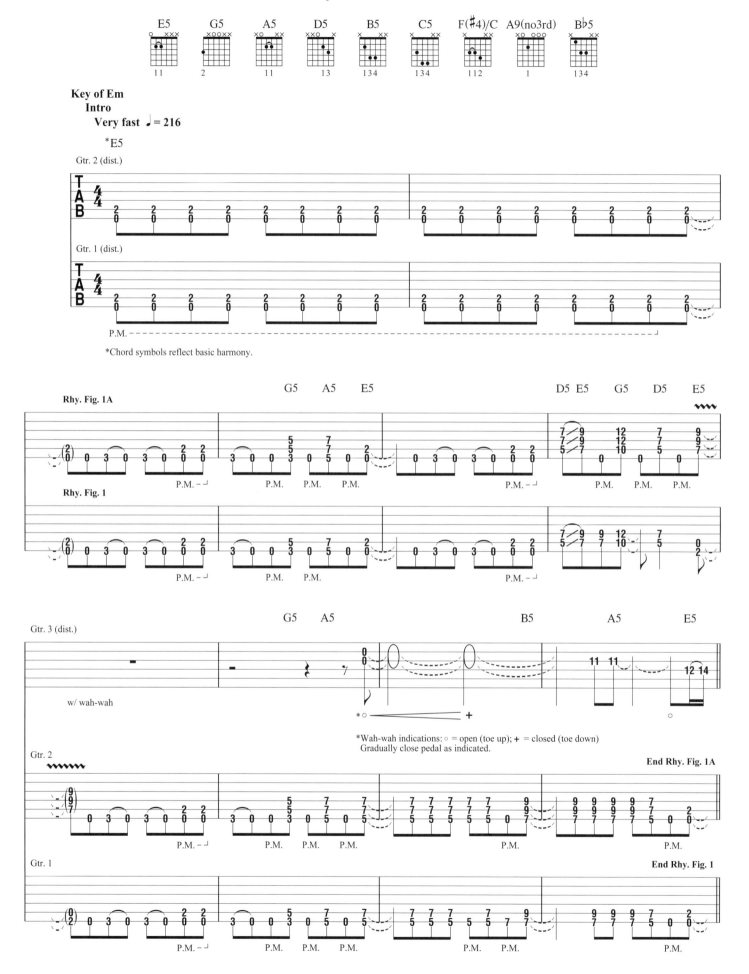

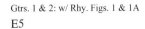

Gtrs. 1 & 2: w/ Rhy. Figs. 1 & 1A

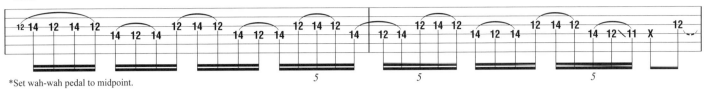

*Gtr. 3

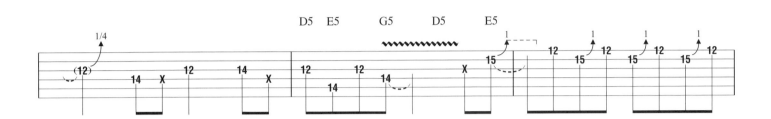

*Set wah-wah pedal to midpoint.

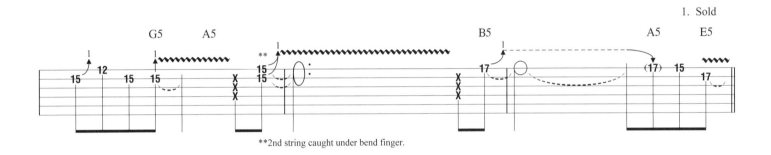

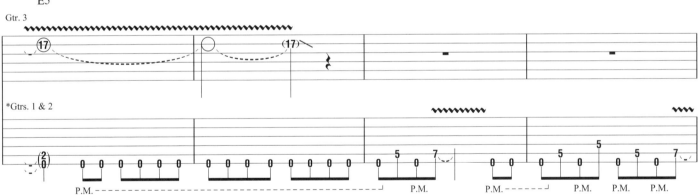

**2nd string caught under bend finger.

1. Sold

Verse

Gtr. 3 tacet

my soul and signed my name in blood. Stole

Gtr. 3

*Gtrs. 1 & 2

P.M. P.M. P.M. P.M. P.M.

*Composite arrangement

it back, now pray-ing in the dark. Fooled

Gtrs. 1 & 2

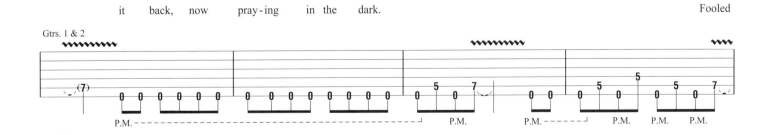

P.M. P.M. P.M. P.M. P.M.

the   Dev - il,   beg-ging   for   a   fight.   Count

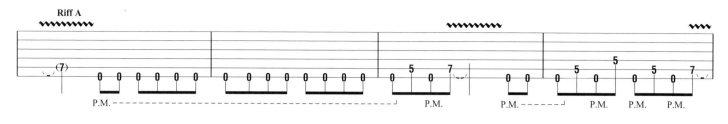

the   dol - lars,   make your   bet to - night.

B5

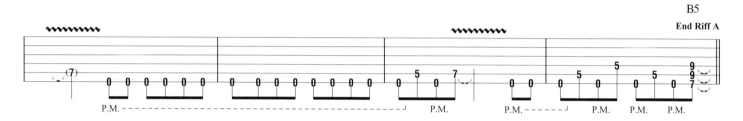

𝄋 Chorus

Feel strong like an   oiled ma - chine.   All the an - ger boils   with - in.

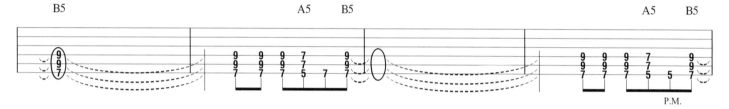

Move it,   give in,   the high   rol - lers   are   in.   I get

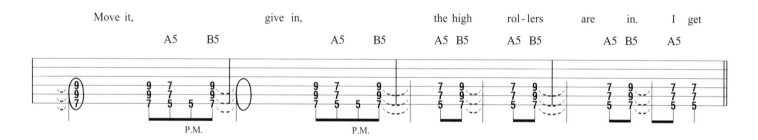

Chorus
Half-time feel

groov - y,   now   turn   it on and   fight.   Seal   the deal,

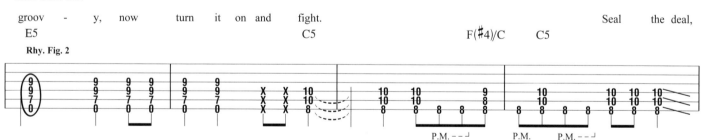

and let's   boog - ie   for a   while.   Let's   get

End Rhy. Fig. 2

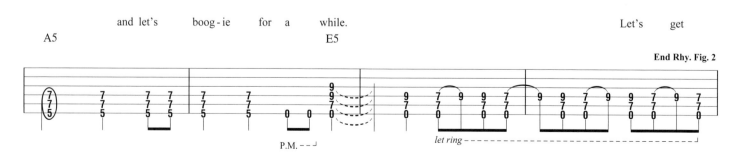

groov - y,   burn - ing out with   rage.   Seal   the deal,

C5   F(♯4)/C   C5

Rhy. Fig. 3

P.M. - - -   P.M.   P.M. - - -

End half-time feel

and let's   do it   all a - gain.

A5   E5

Gtr. 3

w/ wah-wah

Gtrs. 1 & 2   **End Rhy. Fig. 3**

P.M. - - -

let ring -

Guitar Solo

Gtrs. 1 & 2: w/ Rhy. Figs. 1 & 1A

E5   G5 A5 E5   D5 E5   G5 D5 E5

Gtr. 3

*Set wah-wah pedal to midpoint.

3   3   3   3   3

2. Knuck -

G5   A5   B5   A5   E5

1/4

Verse

Gtrs. 1 & 2: w/ Riff A   Gtr. 3 tacet

- les crushed, my   eyes no long-er   see.   I paid

E5

65

the price and | fed the fam - i - ly.

✛ Coda

and let's do it all a - gain.

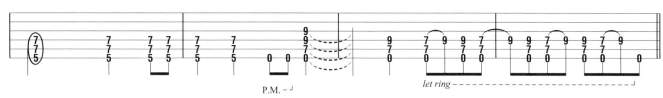

Interlude

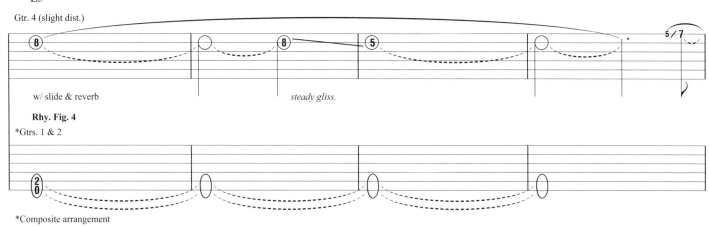

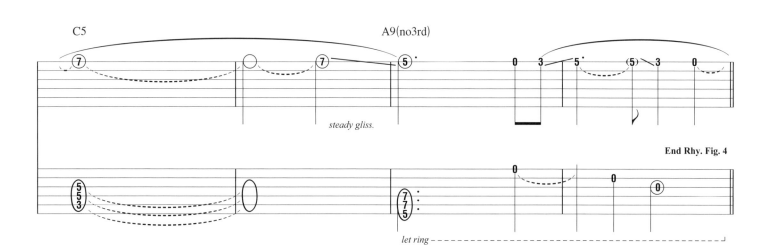

Bridge

Gtrs. 1 & 2: w/ Rhy. Fig. 4 (2 times)

Sing hal - le - lu - jah, the Dev - il in dis - guise.

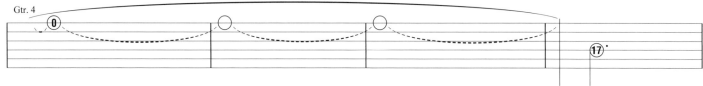

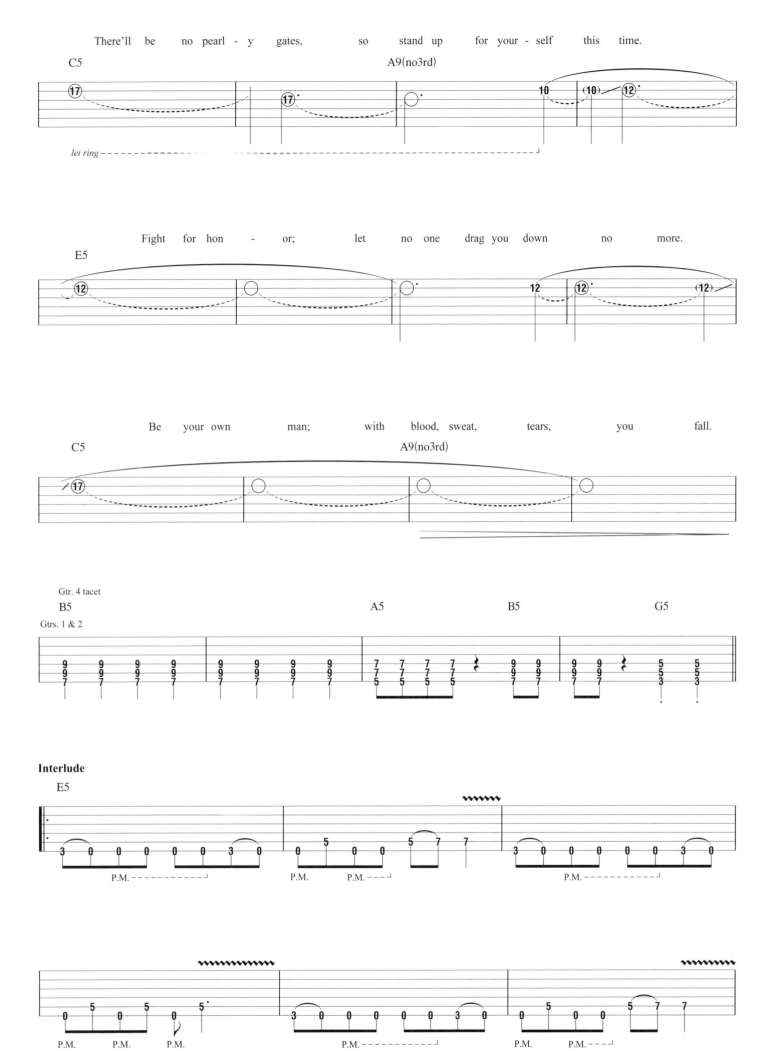

Interlude

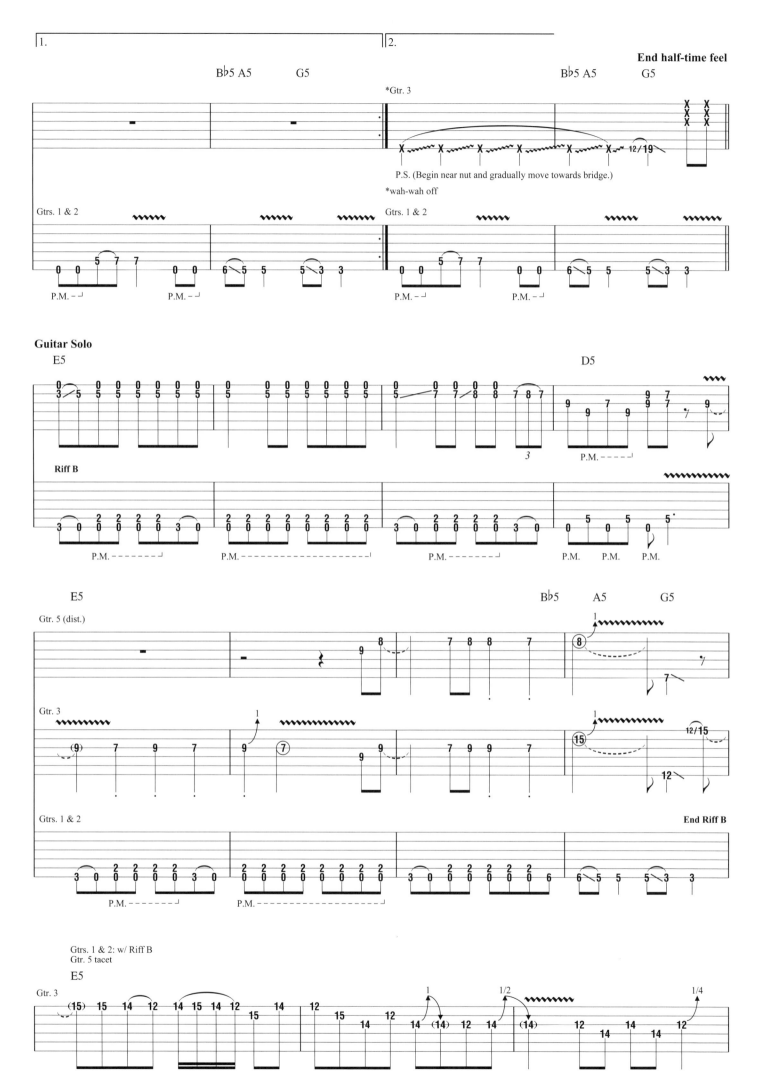

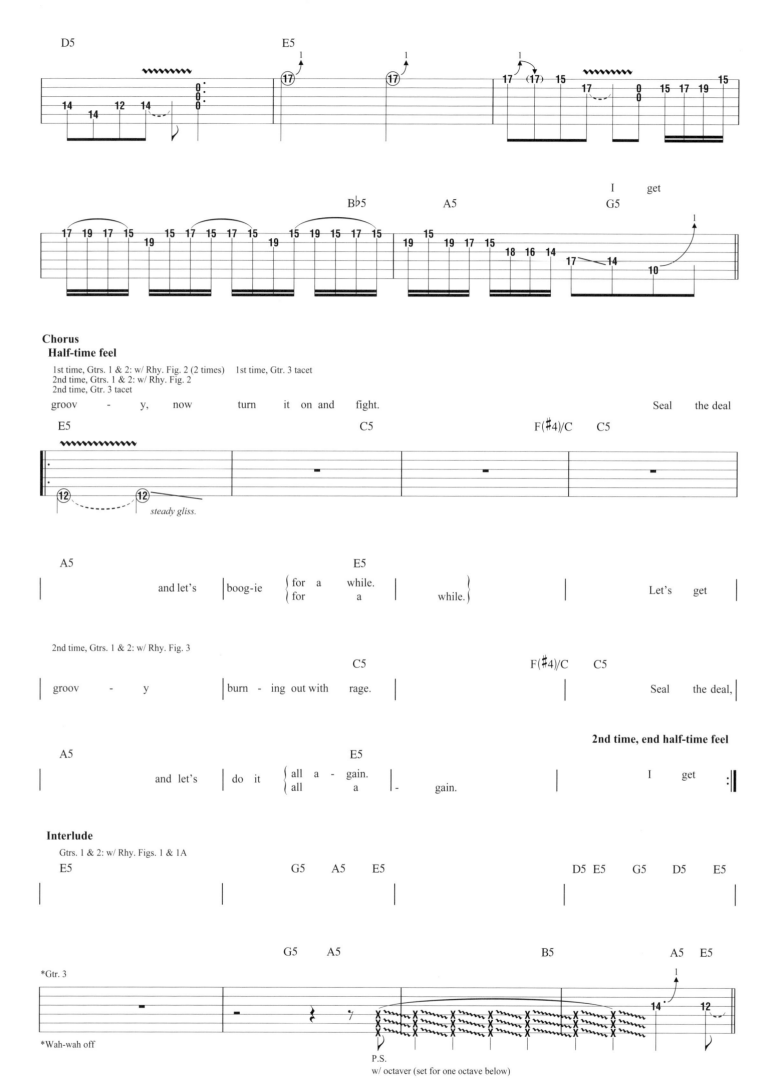

Chorus
Half-time feel

1st time, Grs. 1 & 2: w/ Rhy. Fig. 2 (2 times)   1st time, Gtr. 3 tacet
2nd time, Grs. 1 & 2: w/ Rhy. Fig. 2
2nd time, Gtr. 3 tacet

groov - y,   now   turn   it   on and   fight.   Seal   the deal

and let's | boog-ie { for a   while. | } | Let's   get |
                       { for   a   while. | while.} |

2nd time, Grs. 1 & 2: w/ Rhy. Fig. 3

groov - y | burn - ing out with   rage. | | Seal   the deal, |

2nd time, end half-time feel

and let's | do it { all a - gain. | | I   get |:||
                    { all   a |- gain. |

Interlude
Grs. 1 & 2: w/ Rhy. Figs. 1 & 1A

*Gtr. 3

*Wah-wah off

P.S.
w/ octaver (set for one octave below)

Outro-Guitar Solo

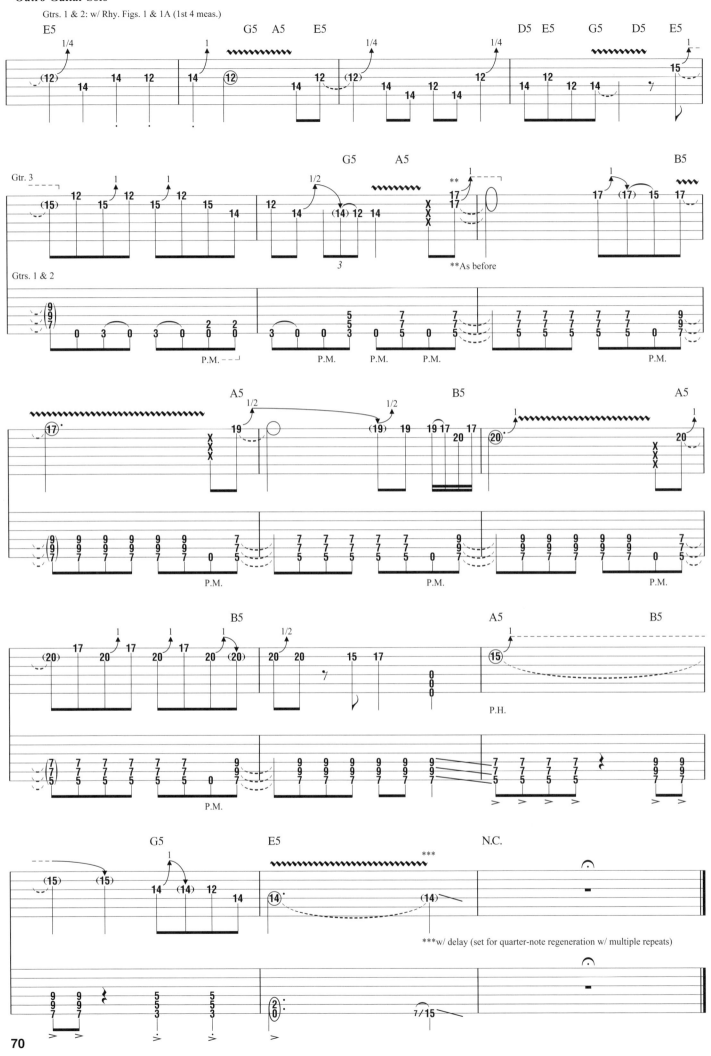

Battleship Chains

Words and Music by Terry Anderson

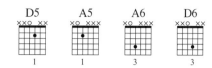

Gtrs. 1, 2 & 4: Tune down 1/2 step:
(low to high) Eb-Ab-Db-Gb-Bb-Eb

Gtr. 3: Open A tuning, down 1/2 step:
(low to high) Eb-Ab-Eb-Ab-C-Eb

Key of D
Intro
Moderately fast ♩ = 130

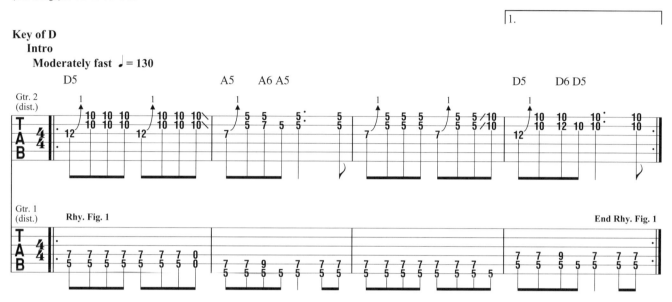

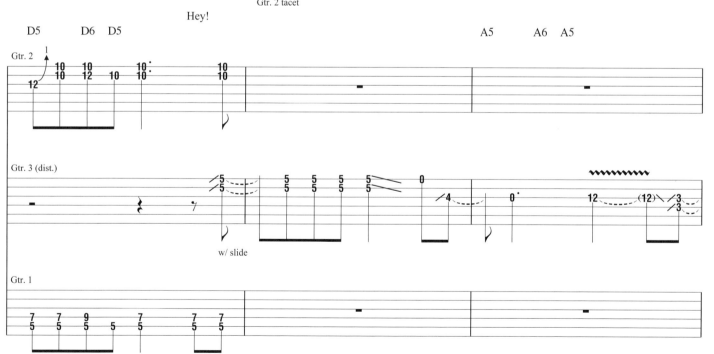

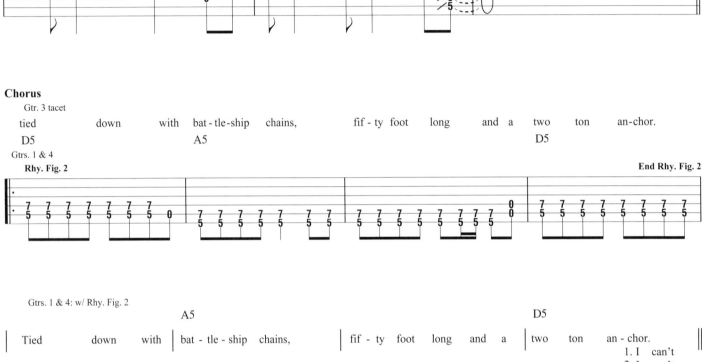

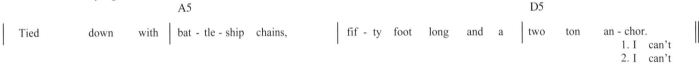

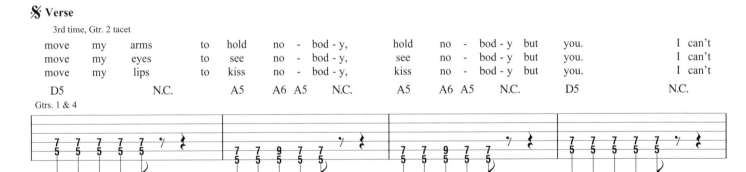

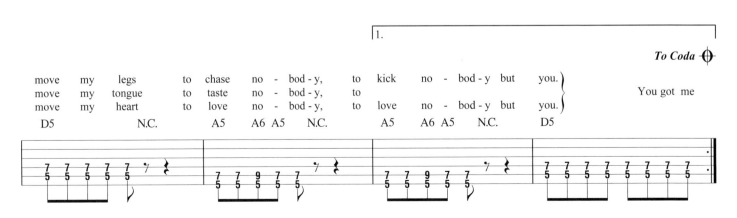

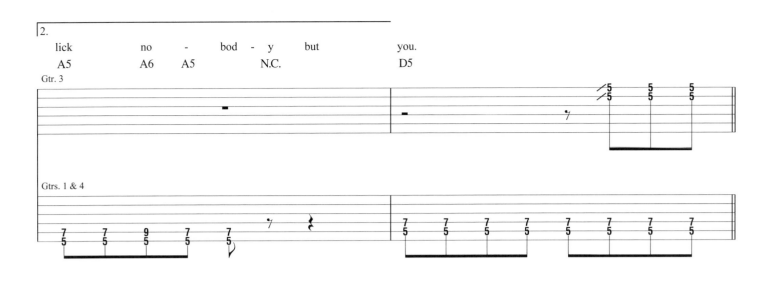

lick   no -   bod -   y   but   you.

Guitar Solo

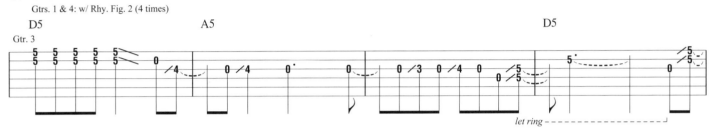

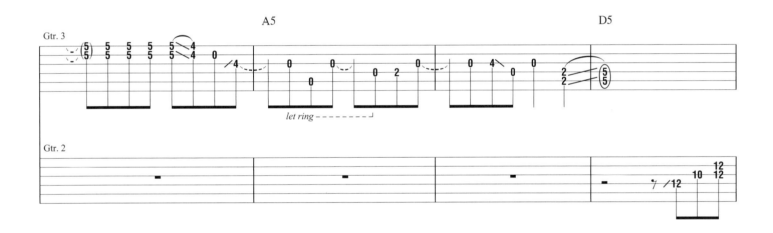

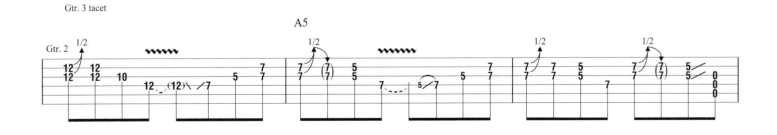

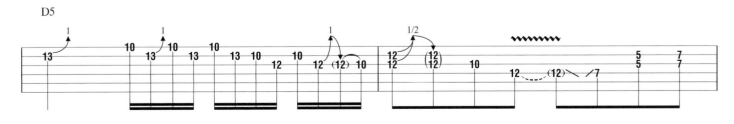

3. I can't

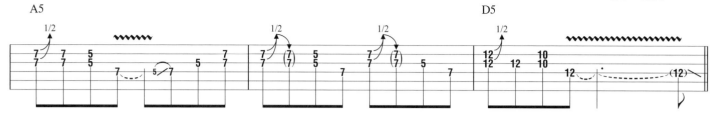

⊕ **Coda**

Chorus

Gtrs. 1 & 4: w/ Rhy. Fig. 2 (2 times)

D5	A5	D5
tied down with	bat - tle - ship chains,	fif - ty foot long and a	two ton an - chor.

Tied down with bat - tle - ship chains, fif - ty foot long and a two ton an - chor.

You got me

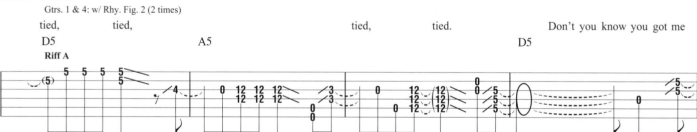

Outro-Chorus

Gtrs. 1 & 4: w/ Rhy. Fig. 2 (2 times)

tied, tied, tied, tied. Don't you know you got me

tied, tied, tied, tied? Ba - by, don't you know you got me

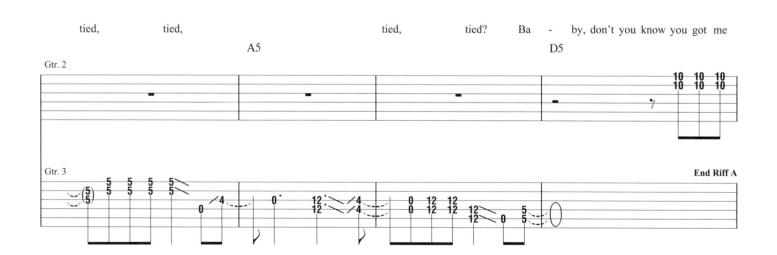

74

Gtrs. 1 & 4: w/ Rhy. Fig. 1 (3 1/2 times)
Gtr. 3 tacet

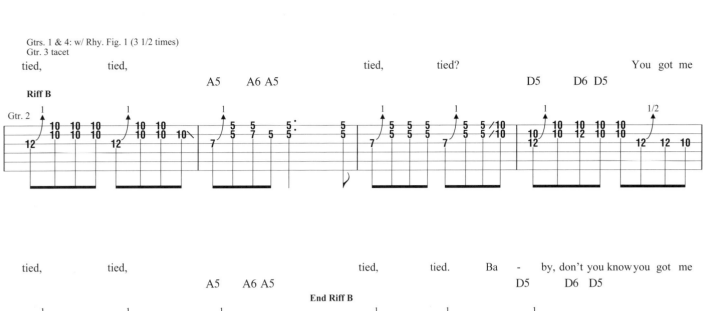

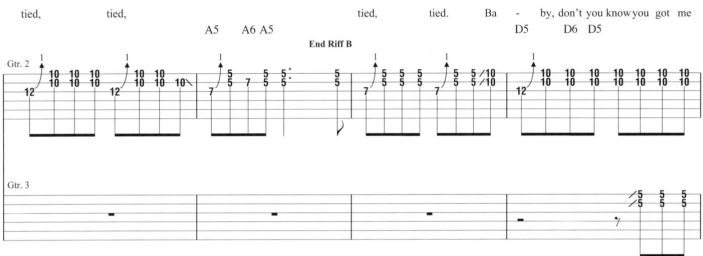

Gtr. 2: w/ Riff B
Gtr. 3: w/ Riff A

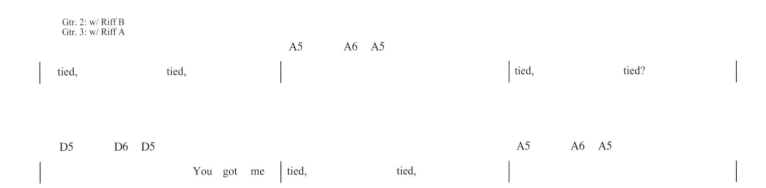

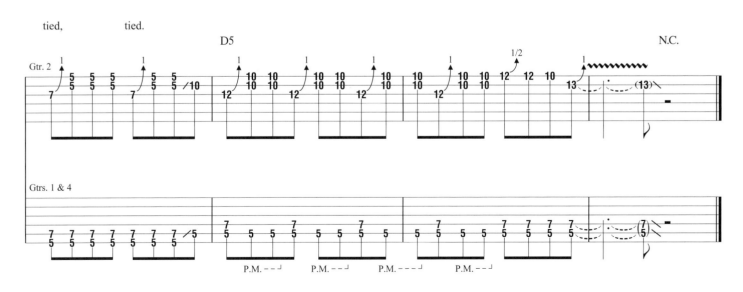

You Will Know

Words and Music by Michael Poulsen, Jon Larsen and Rob Caggiano

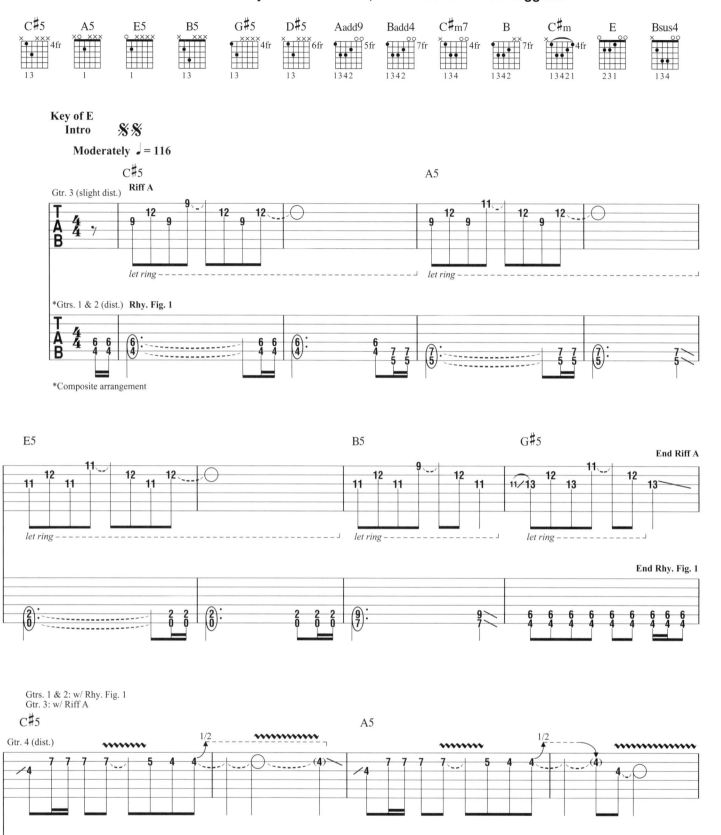

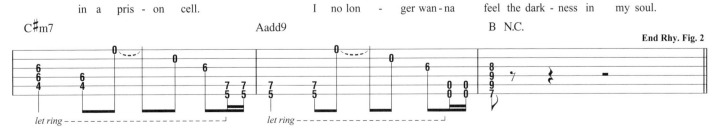

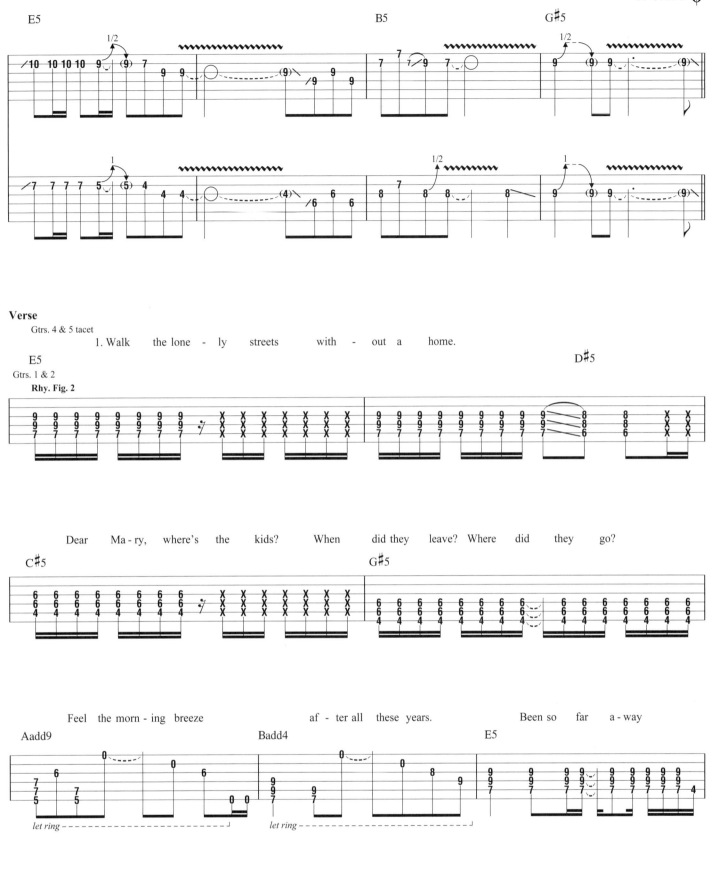

Verse

Gtrs. 4 & 5 tacet

1. Walk the lone - ly streets with - out a home.

Dear Ma - ry, where's the kids? When did they leave? Where did they go?

Feel the morn - ing breeze af - ter all these years. Been so far a - way

in a pris - on cell. I no lon - ger wan - na feel the dark - ness in my soul.

Chorus

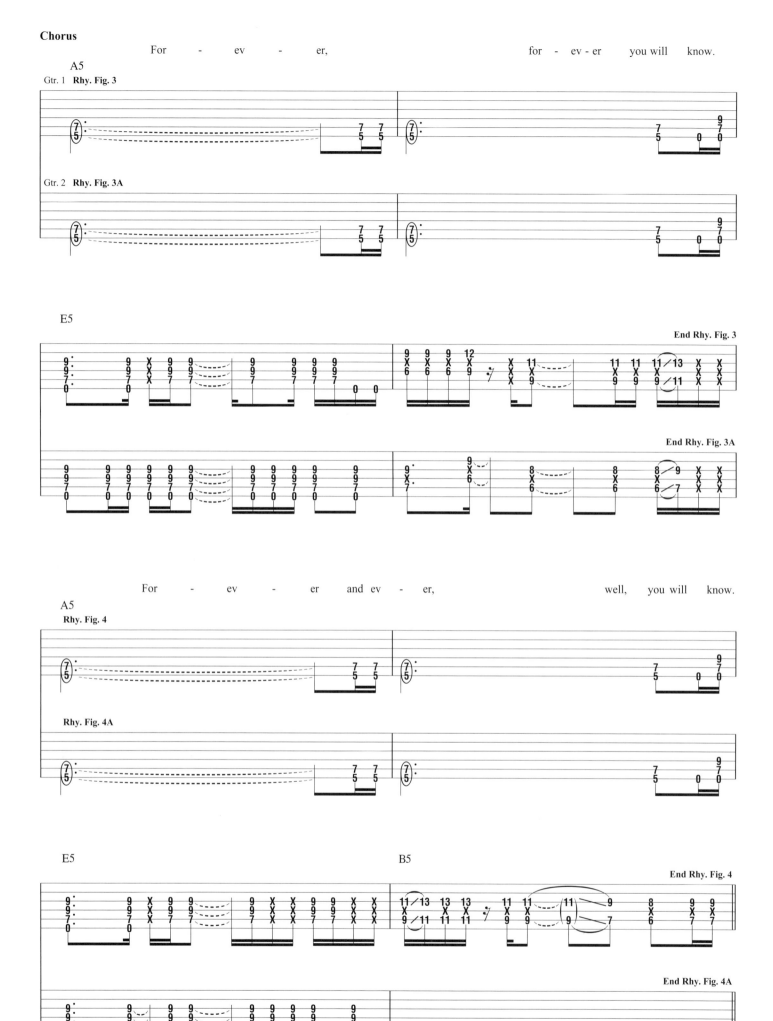

Verse

Gtrs. 1 & 2: w/ Rhy. Fig. 2

E5   **D#5**   **C#5**

Here I sit a-gain, lost | at your place. | I brought the flow-ers that I |

G#5   **Aadd9**

know you like for you, my dear. | All the mem-o-ries |

Badd4   **E5**   **C#m7**

af-ter all these years | could-n't find a way, | nev-er been the same. |

Aadd9   **B   N.C.**

I no lon-ger wan-na | feel the dark-ness in my soul. ‖

𝄋 Chorus

Gtrs. 1 & 2: w/ Rhy. Figs. 3 & 3A (3 times)

A5   **E5**

For - ev - er, | for - ev - er you will know. |

A5   **E5**

For - ev - er and ev | - er, well, you will know. |

To Coda 1 ⊕

A5   **E5**

For - ev - er, | for - ev - er you will know. |

Gtrs. 1 & 2: w/ Rhy. Figs. 4 & 4A

A5   **E5**   **B5**

For - ev - er and ev | - er, well, you will know. ‖

Guitar Solo

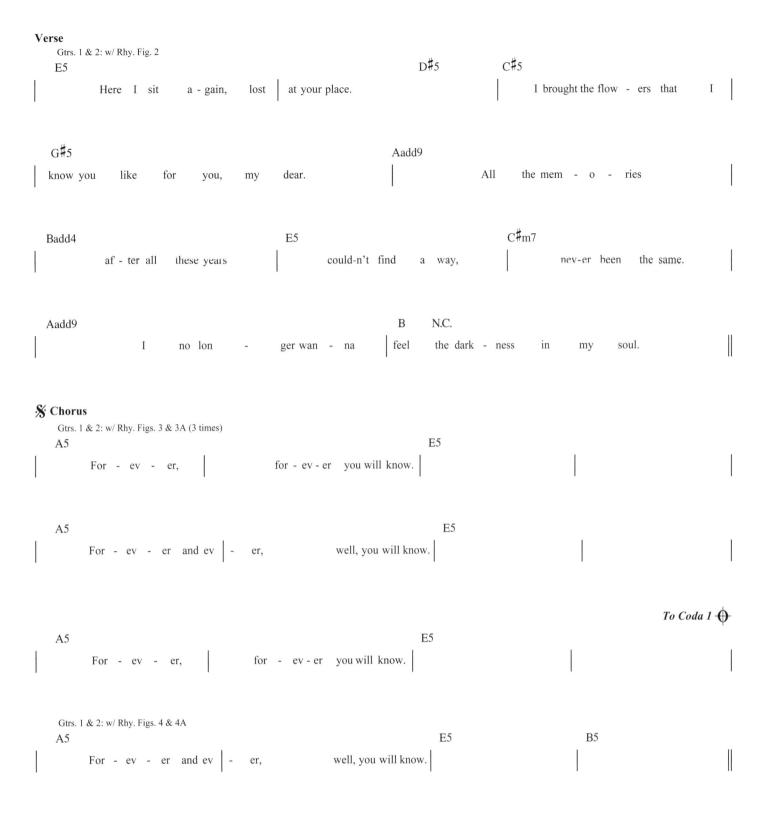

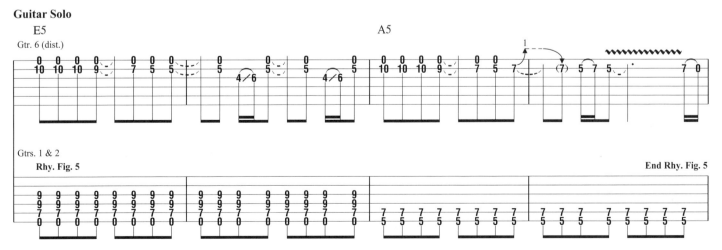

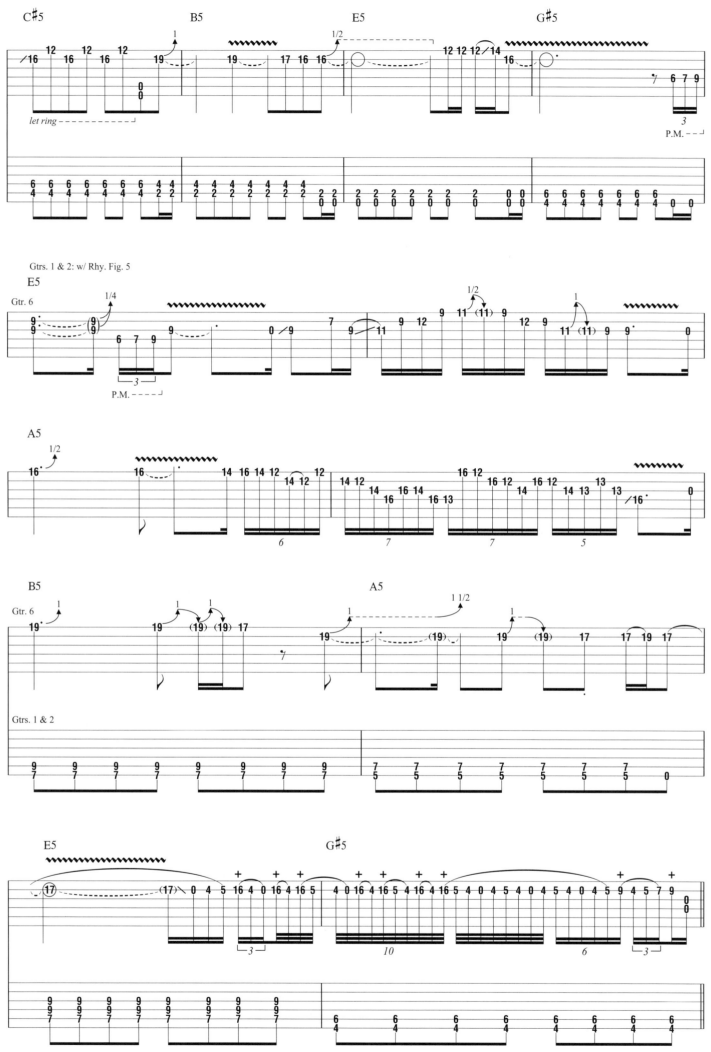

Bridge

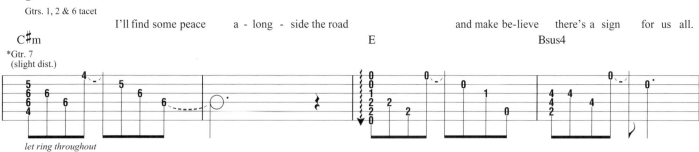

let ring throughout

*Two gtrs. arr. for one

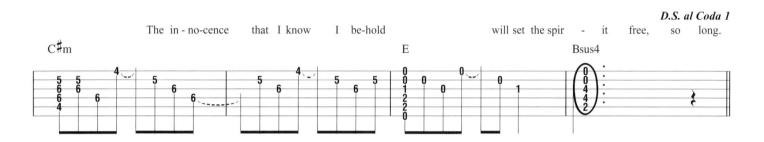

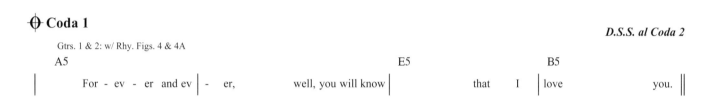

⊕ Coda 1

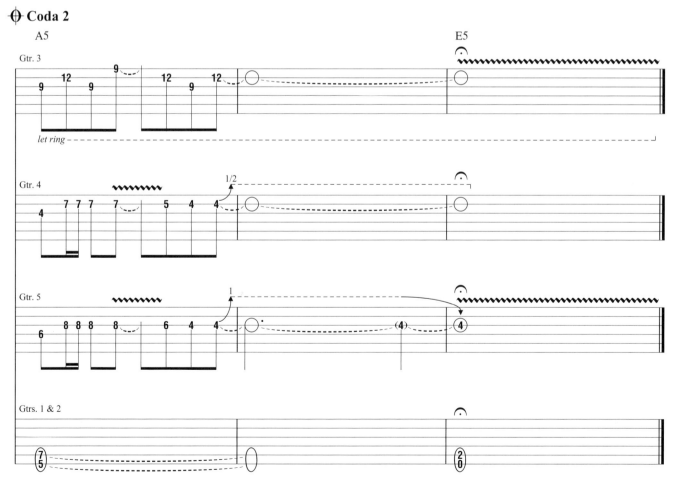

The Loa's Crossroad

Words and Music by Michael Poulsen, Jon Larsen and Rob Caggiano

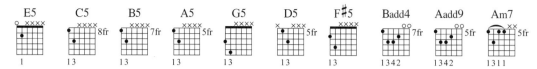

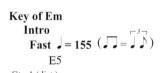

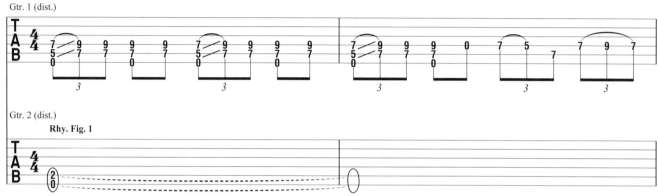

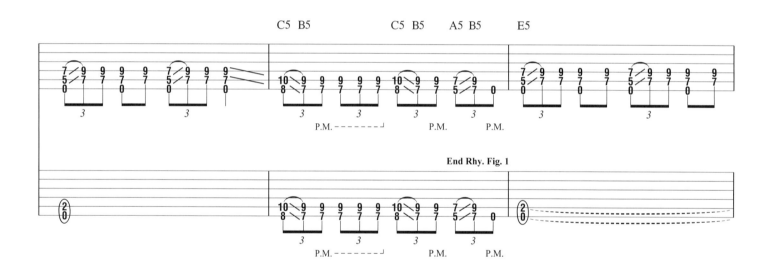

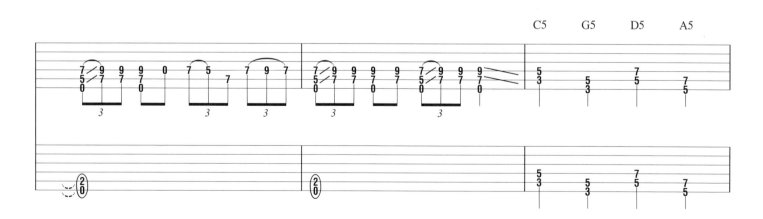

E5

Gtrs.
1 & 2 **Rhy. Fig. 2**

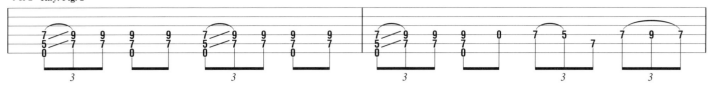

C5 B5   C5 B5   A5 B5   E5

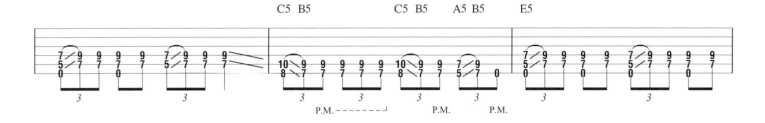

P.M. - - - - - - -   P.M.   P.M.

C5   G5   D5   A5

End Rhy. Fig. 2

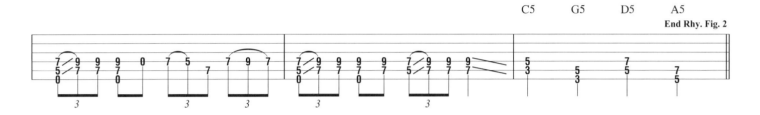

Verse

Gtrs. 1 & 2 tacet

1. Breath - ing,   breath - ing   the   air   from   the   dead.
2. Hear   me,   hear   me,   Bar - on   Sam - e - di.

F#5   A5

Gtrs. 3 & 4 (dist.)

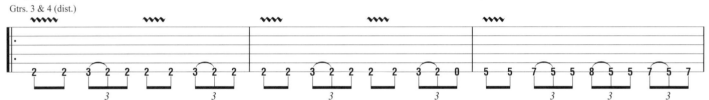

The   stench   of   his   soil,   the   sound   of   him   walk - ing   his
Get   me   a - way   from   this   Lo - a,   I'm   down   on   my

E5   F#5

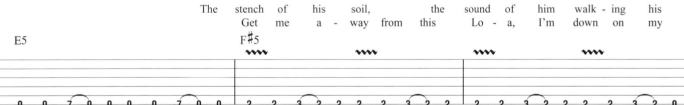

cane.
knees.

A5   E5

Gtr. 3

Gtr. 4

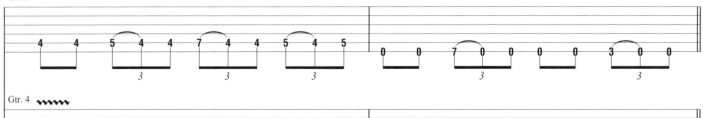

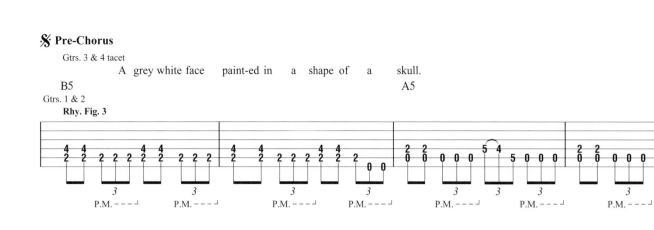

𝄋 Pre-Chorus

Gtrs. 3 & 4 tacet

A grey white face   paint-ed in   a   shape of   a   skull.   A

B5

Gtrs. 1 & 2

Rhy. Fig. 3

End Rhy. Fig. 3

A5

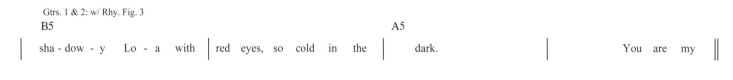

Gtrs. 1 & 2: w/ Rhy. Fig. 3

B5   **A5**

sha - dow - y   Lo - a   with │ red eyes, so   cold   in   the │ dark. │   You   are   my ‖

Chorus

call   of   the   day,   pray - ing   to   o - pen   the   gate.   You've been

E5   **Badd4**   **D5**   **Aadd9**

Rhy. Fig. 4   **End Rhy. Fig. 4**

Gtrs. 1 & 2

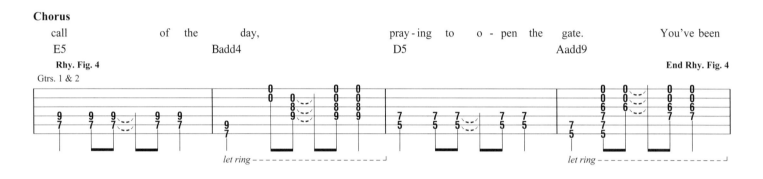

let ring ─────────────────┐   *let ring* ─────────────────┐

fooled   by   Ma - rie.   For   years we've been   seal - in'   the

E5   **Badd4**   **D5**

To Coda ⊕

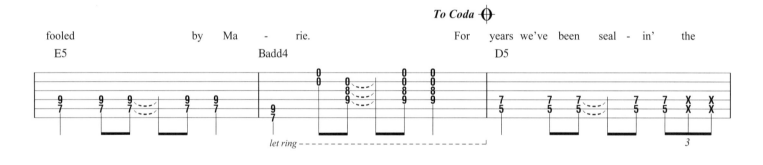

let ring ─────────────────────────────┐

deal.   You,   for   im - mor - tal - i -

F♯5   **C5   G5   D5   A5**

Rhy. Fig. 5   **End Rhy. Fig. 5**

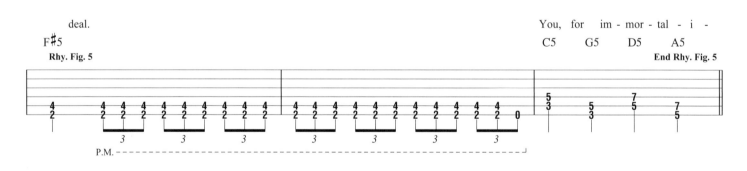

P.M. ───┘

│1.

Interlude

Gtr. 1: w/ Rhy. Fig. 2 (1st 4 meas.)
Gtr. 2: w/ Rhy. Fig. 1

E5   **C5 B5**   **C5 B5   A5 B5**

ty.   │   │   │   ‖

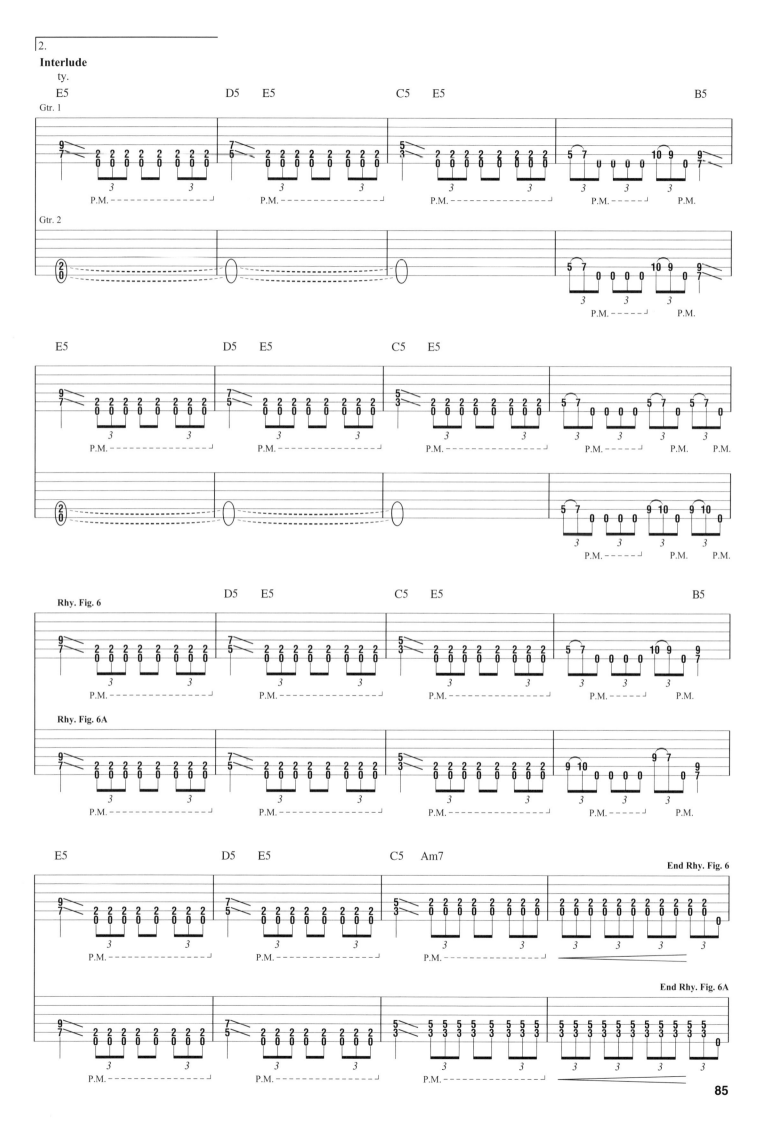

F#5
Gtrs. 1 & 2   E5

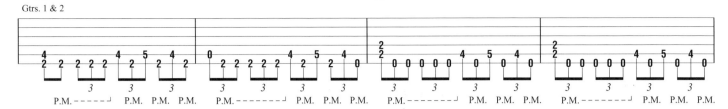

F#5   E5

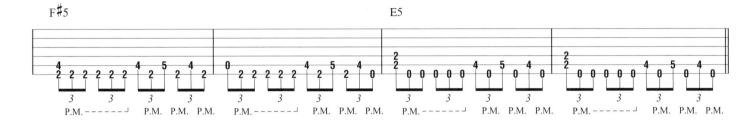

Guitar Solo

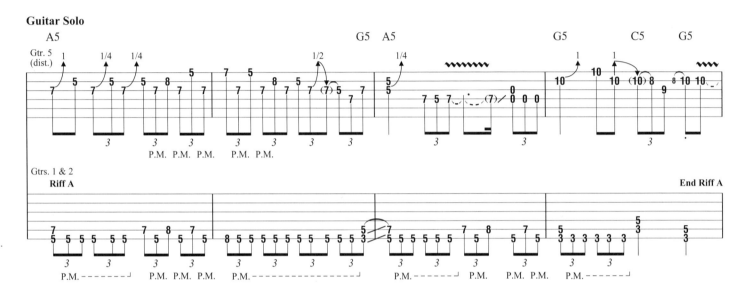

Gtrs. 1 & 2
Riff A   **End Riff A**

Gtrs. 1 & 2: w/ Riff A

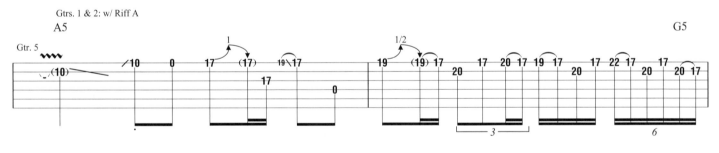

*3rd string caught under bend finger.

Interlude
Gtrs. 1 & 2: w/ Rhy. Figs. 6 & 6A   Gtr. 5 tacet

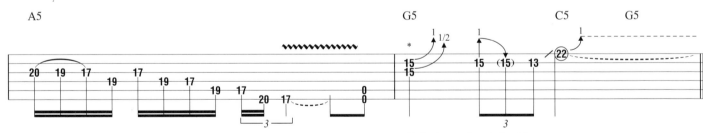

RECORDED VERSIONS®

The Best Note-For-Note Transcriptions Available

AUTHENTIC TRANSCRIPTIONS WITH NOTES AND TABLATURE

14037551	AC/DC – Backtracks $32.99
00690178	Alice in Chains – Acoustic $19.95
00694865	Alice in Chains – Dirt $19.95
00690958	Duane Allman Guitar Anthology $24.99
00694932	Allman Brothers Band – Volume 1 ....$24.95
00694933	Allman Brothers Band – Volume 2 ....$24.95
00694934	Allman Brothers Band – Volume 3 ....$24.95
00123558	Arctic Monkeys – AM $22.99
00690609	Audioslave $19.95
00690820	Avenged Sevenfold – City of Evil $24.95
00691065	Avenged Sevenfold – Waking the Fallen $22.99
00123140	The Avett Brothers Guitar Collection $22.99
00690503	Beach Boys – Very Best of $19.95
00690489	Beatles – 1 ....$24.99
00694832	Beatles – For Acoustic Guitar $22.99
00691014	Beatles Rock Band $34.99
00694914	Beatles – Rubber Soul $22.99
00694863	Beatles – Sgt. Pepper's Lonely Hearts Club Band $22.99
00110193	Beatles – Tomorrow Never Knows $22.99
00690110	Beatles – White Album (Book 1) $19.95
00691043	Jeff Beck – Wired $19.99
00692385	Chuck Berry $22.99
00690835	Billy Talent $19.95
00147787	Best of the Black Crowes $19.99
00690901	Best of Black Sabbath $19.95
14042759	Black Sabbath – 13 ....$19.99
00690831	blink-182 – Greatest Hits $19.95
00148544	Michael Bloomfield Guitar Anthology $24.99
00158600	Joe Bonamassa – Blues of Desperation $22.99
00690913	Boston $19.95
00690491	David Bowie – Best of $19.95
00690873	Breaking Benjamin – Phobia $19.95
00141446	Best of Lenny Breau $19.99
00690451	Jeff Buckley – Collection $24.95
00690957	Bullet for My Valentine – Scream Aim Fire ...$22.99
00691159	The Cars – Complete Greatest Hits $22.99
00691079	Best of Johnny Cash $22.99
00690590	Eric Clapton – Anthology $29.95
00690415	Clapton Chronicles – Best of Eric Clapton ...$18.95
00690936	Eric Clapton – Complete Clapton $29.99
00694869	Eric Clapton – Unplugged $22.95
00138731	Eric Clapton & Friends – The Breeze $22.99
00690162	The Clash – Best of $19.95
00101916	Eric Church – Chief $22.99
00690828	Coheed & Cambria – Good Apollo I'm Burning Star, IV, Vol. 1: From Fear Through the Eyes of Madness $19.95
00141704	Jesse Cook – Works Vol. 1 ....$19.99
00127184	Best of Robert Cray $19.99
00690819	Creedence Clearwater Revival – Best of $22.95
00690648	The Very Best of Jim Croce $19.95
00690613	Crosby, Stills & Nash – Best of $22.95
00691171	Cry of Love – Brother $22.99
00690967	Death Cab for Cutie – Narrow Stairs $22.99
00690289	Deep Purple – Best of $19.99
00690784	Def Leppard – Best of $22.99
00692240	Bo Diddley $19.99
00122443	Dream Theater $24.99
14041903	Bob Dylan for Guitar Tab $19.99
00139220	Tommy Emmanuel – Little by Little $24.99
00691186	Evanescence $22.99
00691181	Five Finger Death Punch – American Capitalist ...$22.99
00690664	Fleetwood Mac – Best of $19.95
00690870	Flyleaf $19.95
00690808	Foo Fighters – In Your Honor $19.95
00691115	Foo Fighters – Wasting Light $22.99
00690805	Robben Ford – Best of $22.99
00120220	Robben Ford – Guitar Anthology $24.99
00694920	Free – Best of $19.95

00690943	The Goo Goo Dolls – Greatest Hits Volume 1: The Singles $22.95
00691190	Best of Peter Green $19.99
00113073	Green Day – ¡Uno! $21.99
00116846	Green Day – ¡Dos! $21.99
00118259	Green Day – ¡Tré! $21.99
00694854	Buddy Guy – Damn Right, I've Got the Blues ..$19.95
00690840	Ben Harper – Both Sides of the Gun $19.95
00694798	George Harrison – Anthology $19.95
00690841	Scott Henderson – Blues Guitar Collection ...$19.95
00692930	Jimi Hendrix – Are You Experienced? $24.95
00692931	Jimi Hendrix – Axis: Bold As Love $22.95
00692932	Jimi Hendrix – Electric Ladyland $24.95
00690017	Jimi Hendrix – Live at Woodstock $24.95
00690602	Jimi Hendrix – Smash Hits $24.99
00119619	Jimi Hendrix – People, Hell and Angels $22.99
00691152	West Coast Seattle Boy: The Jimi Hendrix Anthology $29.99
00691332	Jimi Hendrix – Winterland (Highlights) $22.99
00690793	John Lee Hooker Anthology $24.99
00121961	Imagine Dragons – Night Visions $22.99
00690688	Incubus – A Crow Left of the Murder $19.95
00690790	Iron Maiden Anthology $24.99
00690684	Jethro Tull – Aqualung $19.95
00690814	John5 – Songs for Sanity $19.95
00690751	John5 – Vertigo $19.95
00122439	Jack Johnson – From Here to Now to You ...$22.99
00690271	Robert Johnson – New Transcriptions $24.95
00699131	Janis Joplin – Best of $19.95
00690427	Judas Priest – Best of $22.99
00120814	Killswitch Engage – Disarm the Descent $22.99
00124869	Albert King with Stevie Ray Vaughan – In Session $22.99
00694903	Kiss – Best of $24.95
00690355	Kiss – Destroyer $16.95
00690834	Lamb of God – Ashes of the Wake $19.95
00690875	Lamb of God – Sacrament $19.95
00114563	The Lumineers $22.99
00690955	Lynyrd Skynyrd – All-Time Greatest Hits ...$22.99
00694954	Lynyrd Skynyrd – New Best of $19.95
00690754	Marilyn Manson – Lest We Forget $19.95
00694956	Bob Marley – Legend $19.95
00694945	Bob Marley – Songs of Freedom $24.95
00139168	Pat Martino – Guitar Anthology $24.99
00129105	John McLaughlin Guitar Tab Anthology $24.99
00120080	Don McLean – Songbook $19.95
00694951	Megadeth – Rust in Peace $22.95
00691185	Megadeth – Th1rt3en $22.99
00690951	Megadeth – United Abominations $22.99
00690505	John Mellencamp – Guitar Collection $19.95
00690646	Pat Metheny – One Quiet Night $19.95
00690558	Pat Metheny – Trio: 99>00 ....$24.99
00118836	Pat Metheny – Unity Band $22.99
00690040	Steve Miller Band – Young Hearts $19.95
00119338	Ministry Guitar Tab Collection $24.99
00102591	Wes Montgomery Guitar Anthology $24.99
00691070	Mumford & Sons – Sigh No More $22.99
00151195	Muse – Drones $19.99
00694883	Nirvana – Nevermind $19.95
00690026	Nirvana – Unplugged in New York $19.95
00690807	The Offspring – Greatest Hits $19.95
00694847	Ozzy Osbourne – Best of $22.95
00690399	Ozzy Osbourne – Ozzman Cometh $22.99
00690933	Best of Brad Paisley $22.95
00690995	Brad Paisley – Play: The Guitar Album $24.99
00694855	Pearl Jam – Ten $22.99
00690439	A Perfect Circle – Mer De Noms $19.95
00690499	Tom Petty – Definitive Guitar Collection ...$19.95
00121933	Pink Floyd – Acoustic Guitar Collection ...$22.99
00690428	Pink Floyd – Dark Side of the Moon $19.95
00690789	Poison – Best of $19.95
00690670	Queen – Greatest Hits $24.95
00690670	Queensryche – Very Best of $19.95
00109303	Radiohead Guitar Anthology $24.99

00694910	Rage Against the Machine $19.95
00119834	Rage Against the Machine – Guitar Anthology .$22.99
00690055	Red Hot Chili Peppers – Blood Sugar Sex Magik $19.95
00690584	Red Hot Chili Peppers – By the Way $19.95
00691166	Red Hot Chili Peppers – I'm with You $22.99
00690852	Red Hot Chili Peppers – Stadium Arcadium .$24.95
00690511	Django Reinhardt – Definitive Collection ...$19.95
00690779	Relient K – MMHMM $19.95
14043417	Rodrigo y Gabriela – 9 Dead Alive $19.99
00690631	Rolling Stones – Guitar Anthology $27.95
00694976	Rolling Stones – Some Girls $22.95
00690264	The Rolling Stones – Tattoo You $19.95
00690685	David Lee Roth – Eat 'Em and Smile $19.95
00690942	David Lee Roth and the Songs of Van Halen ...$19.95
00151826	Royal Blood $22.99
00690031	Santana's Greatest Hits $19.95
00128870	Matt Schofield Guitar Tab Collection $22.99
00690566	Scorpions – Best of $22.95
00690604	Bob Seger – Guitar Collection $22.99
00138870	Ed Sheeran – X $19.99
00690803	Kenny Wayne Shepherd Band – Best of $19.95
00151178	Kenny Wayne Shepherd – Ledbetter Heights (20th Anniversary Edition) $19.99
00122218	Skillet – Rise $22.99
00691114	Slash – Guitar Anthology $24.99
00690813	Slayer – Guitar Collection $19.95
00120004	Steely Dan – Best of $24.95
00694921	Steppenwolf – Best of $22.95
00690655	Mike Stern – Best of $19.95
00690520	Styx Guitar Collection $19.95
00120081	Sublime $19.95
00120122	Sublime – 40oz. to Freedom $19.95
00690767	Switchfoot – The Beautiful Letdown $19.95
00690993	Taylor Swift – Fearless $22.99
00142151	Taylor Swift – 1989 ....$22.99
00115957	Taylor Swift – Red $21.99
00690531	System of a Down – Toxicity $19.95
00694824	James Taylor – Best of $17.95
00690871	Three Days Grace – One-X $19.95
00150209	Trans-Siberian Orchestra Guitar Anthology ...$19.99
00123862	Trivium – Vengeance Falls $22.99
00690683	Robin Trower – Bridge of Sighs $19.95
00660137	Steve Vai – Passion & Warfare $24.95
00110385	Steve Vai – The Story of Light $22.99
00690116	Stevie Ray Vaughan – Guitar Collection $24.95
00660058	Stevie Ray Vaughan – Lightnin' Blues 1983-1987 ....$24.95
00694835	Stevie Ray Vaughan – The Sky Is Crying ...$22.95
00690015	Stevie Ray Vaughan – Texas Flood $19.95
00152161	Doc Watson – Guitar Anthology $22.99
00690071	Weezer (The Blue Album) $19.95
00690966	Weezer – (Red Album) $19.99
00691941	The Who – Acoustic Guitar Collection $22.99
00690447	The Who – Best of $24.95
00122303	Yes Guitar Collection $22.99
00690916	The Best of Dwight Yoakam $19.95
00691020	Neil Young – After the Gold Rush $22.99
00691019	Neil Young – Everybody Knows This Is Nowhere $19.99
00691021	Neil Young – Harvest Moon $22.99
00690905	Neil Young – Rust Never Sleeps $19.99
00690623	Frank Zappa – Over-Nite Sensation $24.99
00121684	ZZ Top – Early Classics $24.99
00690589	ZZ Top Guitar Anthology $24.95